DESIGN THINKING PLCs

Revolutionize
Teacher
Collaboration

Brett Taylor

Design Thinking PLCs: Revolutionize Teacher Collaboration

Copyright © 2020 by Brett Taylor

Published by NewSchool Innovation Consulting LLC
Folsom, CA
www.newschoolinnovation.com

Edited by Jill Kelly
Cover Design by Keith Cappelluti
Author Photo by Jacklyn Carter

Paperback ISBN: 978-1-952307-00-3
Ebook ISBN: 978-1-952307-01-0

NewSchool
Innovation Consulting

This book is accompanied by a free *Design Thinking PLCs Playbook* which contains tools and templates supporting the work presented throughout this book. The playbook is a pdf which can be downloaded at https://www.newschoolinnovation.com/design-thinking-plcs.

The goal of this book is to spread the Design Thinking PLC movement. If you find any of the information useful, please consider leaving a review on Amazon. Educators sharing useful ideas with other educators is how we advance innovation in our field. Thanks!

For the founding faculty of the Phillip J.
Patiño School of Entrepreneurship—
my first Design Thinking PLC

CONTENTS

PART 4: TESTING SOLUTIONS AND REFLECTING

INTRODUCTION

How do you feel when you hear or read the abbreviation *PLC*? When I ask this question of teachers, I get a lot of interesting answers:

- Anger
- Dread
- Boredom
- Discomfort
- Frustration

I hesitated to use *PLC* in the title of my book. I was worried it might scare you away. However, I wrote this book for those of you who have felt those feelings. This book describes how you can change your dreaded PLC into something you love.

Most schools engage in professional learning communities (PLCs) or some form of teacher collaboration. These groups were originally created to support teachers in the goal of improving student learning. But over the years, many PLCs have become compliance-focused. Some of these communities have turned into nothing more than mandated meetings, with forms to fill out and objectives to communicate to administrators.

Even when teachers try to make these meetings work, they often struggle. A lot of teachers are genuinely trying to spend PLC time talking about instruction, but they don't know how to make these conversations meaningful or to connect them to their classrooms. These types of meetings often become a round robin of teachers sharing anecdotes, but not figuring out how to create systemic change or improvement in the classroom.

Sound familiar? You might want to blame PLCs, but PLCs can be so much more than this.

What if you could experience PLCs that do more than check off the compliance box? Instead they could focus completely on students' needs and show direct impact on instruction and learning. PLCs that actually lead to engaged students and improved instruction in the classroom. Even better, what if you could experience real innovation happening in your school? And what if you could feel engaged and excited about it all?

This is what Design Thinking PLCs can do for teacher collaboration.

Design thinking is an innovation process that has been used by organizations for decades. This iterative process focuses on identifying the needs of a user and creating and testing new solutions. It requires collaborative teams to dream up new ideas and design ways to make these ideas a reality. Imagine the excitement of creating a new product, service, or invention. Now think of the power of bringing this iterative process into teacher collaboration. Can you imagine boring meetings becoming exciting design sessions?

When I founded the Phillip J. Patiño School of Entrepreneurship, a high school focused on creating entrepreneurs, I discovered the power of incorporating design thinking into the PLC process. As I felt this magic happen, I began to identify the specific parts of the design thinking process that could be used by any PLC. Now, I've created a system that can empower teachers at any school to take advantage of the ingenuity of design thinking in collaboration. We used the Design Thinking PLC process to prototype and test this solution with teachers, ultimately leading to the tools and teachings in this book.

Teachers who engage in Design Thinking PLCs begin to fully understand the needs of their students, and they can work to creatively meet these needs. This process revolutionizes teacher collaboration and transforms classrooms and students. I have worked with PLCs that have consistently stayed more than an hour past their mandated time because they were so engaged in designing a prototype. I have worked with other teachers who started meeting after school to work on their solution without any prompting from their administrators. They got wrapped up in the process and rediscovered their passion for teaching.

One teacher reacted in this way to Design Thinking PLCs: "I feel like this isn't work. It really is fun." Another teacher said, "My team is working on a whole different level now!"

I promise that if you work with your team to implement this system, you will experience an increased understanding of student needs, an explosion of innovative teaching, and huge increases in teacher and student engagement. I can make this promise because I have seen it happen at multiple school sites that have implemented the Design Thinking PLC system.

Of course, you could continue with the status quo. You could keep counting down the moments until the end of boring meetings. Or you could start making learning more meaningful for your students and make PLCs what they were always supposed to be. Don't miss out on the opportunity to make your school into a "design studio" where student voices lead to amazing learning outcomes through exciting instruction that adapts on the fly. This is an opportunity to help make your PLC into a problem-solving center.

The structures, processes, and tips you will read about in this book are not easy hacks; they require collaborative teams that work together to support student learning. It can be more work to engage your creative muscles in this process, which will stretch your ability as an educator. However, at the same time, you will discover a renewed sense of urgency and reengage in an excitement that may have been lost to you and your team.

If this seems like a good deal, then you can start your own design process. This book will help you reimagine PLCs as Design Thinking PLCs. You will feel the difference.

THE DESIGN THINKING PLC | PART 1

1

PLCs

We sat in a circle and stared at each other. The hour dragged. I knew we were supposed to be doing something, but I wasn't sure what. We had survived a long school day and we were spent. We had an agenda to fill out, so eventually someone started talking about something she was teaching in her classroom. We bantered back and forth about experiences, often complaining about student behaviors more than focusing on instruction or academic achievement. We needed to fill out our paperwork to turn into the administration, so I quickly repeated the things we had talked about and wrote them down, and we concluded the meeting. As we walked away, none of us were sure what we had gained.

Perhaps you have had a similar experience. As a teacher, you may have sat through an excruciatingly boring collaboration feeling as if you could be doing something productive instead. You may also have experienced the power of good teacher collaboration. Some of my PLC moments, both as a teacher and administrator, were electric. There was an excitement about new ideas teachers wanted to try out in their classrooms. Teachers were sharing data collected from students and were working together to figure out how to support students in their areas of weakness. Some PLCs are high-functioning and are making a difference in classrooms.

So why the huge spectrum between laborious teacher collaborations that make you wish you were having your teeth pulled out instead and high-energy meetings where you leave feeling excited about taking on the world of 32 12-year-olds that awaits you tomorrow morning? How come some teacher collaboration seems to work wonders, while other PLCs are going nowhere and feel like wasted time?

Before we get to Design Thinking PLCs, it's important to look at the traditional PLC− what it generally looks like, and what it could be. This context will help you understand the Design Thinking PLC and how you can fit it into your current PLC.

The Intended PLC

The idea of professional learning communities in education has been around since the 1960s. They were created to break down the isolation that exists in a profession where most teachers spend their days as the only adult in a room full of children.

In the early 2000s, the popularity of PLCs grew with the work of Richard DuFour and his colleagues[1]. They created a specific PLC structure that

---

1 Dufour, R. (2004). What is a professional learning community? *Educational Leadership. 61*(8), 6−11.

schools started to adopt around the country. When educators refer to PLCs, they are usually referring to the DuFour PLC, or what I refer to as the traditional PLC.

The traditional PLC was centered on a few important principles. These principles demonstrate the focus of the initial PLC revolution.

Focus on Student Learning

The goal of traditional PLCs was to support student learning. In other words, teachers were not supposed to spend time in PLCs talking about bake sales or recess. The focus was specifically on what students were learning in the classroom. These PLCs were built around three questions meant to focus teacher collaboration on student learning:

- *What do we want students to learn?*
- *How will we know they have learned it?*
- *How will we respond if they haven't learned it?*

Focus on Results

In these traditional PLCs, the success of the PLCs was determined by student results. This meant teachers needed to somehow assess student learning based on the instructional changes they had made as a PLC. The structure required teachers to bring student data to PLC meetings to discuss the effectiveness of past work and to plan next instructional steps.

However, the ultimate measure of student learning was improvement on standards-based exams. You are probably sensing a pattern here. The idea of student learning had a very narrow focus: student achievement, as defined by state testing. Remember, these traditional PLCs were popularized at the same time as the No Child Left Behind federal legislation was being implemented. Multiple choice testing was *the* measure for what was deemed as "student achievement." And one of the reasons for the traditional PLC's rise in popularity is that research showed a correlation between good teacher collaboration and improvement on test scores.

This wasn't the intent of the DuFour PLC, which encouraged formative assessment alongside of summative assessments. But this focus on testing through PLCs became the reality of many schools around the country.

Teacher Collaboration & PLC Progression

Traditional PLCs were built around the idea that teachers could learn together: as teachers collaborated, there would be collective learning and teacher growth. The PLC itself would progress as teachers worked together on student learning issues. After several years, PLCs could become incredible teaching teams that had grown in capacity through shared support and collaborative learning.

These ideas of collaboration and growth demonstrate the true professional learning community. The phrase that built the PLC abbreviation, professional learning communities, can sometimes get lost in the shuffle, but the true intention of PLCs is to be an adult learning community working to create a student learning community.

The REAL Traditional PLC

Most of us have experienced the negative type of PLC I talked about at the beginning of the chapter more often than the intended traditional PLC. Examining the reality of today's PLCs reveals a lot of problems.

Lack of Structure

Many schools today have mandated time for PLCs, but their expectations for the use of that time varies greatly, nor is there a common understanding of what should be happening. Schools also experience changes in administration over the years which can further cause practices to become undefined or misunderstood.

Because of this and other factors, many PLCs lack a real structure. Teachers get together and work together, but there is no rhyme or reason to what they are doing. Some teachers find themselves just sitting in a group and talking. Others have a set plan or agenda, but the subjects vary from week to week. Any structure that exists is self-imposed. What's more, with the same school, different PLCs' structure and purpose might look very different.

What over How

Many traditional PLCs spin their wheels focusing on what to teach and not how to teach it. There are many reasons for this, including the following:

- Teachers are most comfortable with content
- It's easier to focus on curriculum than pedagogical skill
- Tests are built around content (even though student performance is largely based on learning)
- Teachers don't know how to tackle how to teach

This leads to a lot of unit planning, curriculum mapping, etc. None of these are bad things, unless they are the only things a PLC focuses on. Ultimately, students can only learn when we get past the *what* they need to learn to the *how* we can effectively teach it to them, but many PLCs never get there.

Focus on Everything other than Student Learning

We all need to vent sometimes. But PLCs that consistently become gripe fests aren't very productive. I once had a friend who called a specific

PLC the *No-Hope Bar and Grill*. I get it, and I admit to having partici-pated in these "venting sessions" in the past. Teaching is a stressful profes-sion. Other teachers are often the only other people on the planet who understand what you have to go through every day. Downloading your frustrations can be healthy when necessary. It just doesn't usually lead to improved professional practice.

Aside from complaining about students or the administration, PLCs can also become places where planning for extra-curricular activities takes precedence over planning for instruction. Even focusing on classroom management or student behavior doesn't quite get us to the instructional strategies we need to adopt to make a difference in the classroom.

Ideas over Action

Sometimes great ideas are born in PLCs. I have left some sessions invig-orated by all of the amazing ideas we came up with. I couldn't wait to get started. And then… well, they just stayed ideas. We didn't really do anything with them.

Ideas are an important part of the PLC. The Design Thinking PLC has an entire ideation stage. But those ideas need to lead somewhere. They need to lead to action and, ultimately, to results to create real change.

PLCs can also become stagnant. There may be some real excitement in a single ideation meeting, but if the same thing continues to happen every week, the process doesn't go anywhere and loses steam. Teachers will get burnt out and frustrated because none of the ideas ever come to fruition.

Lack of Student Data

Many traditional PLCs do not focus on student data. There are a few reasons for this:

- They aren't collaboratively planning to collect student data.
- They only talk about what to teach not how to measure it.
- Teachers forget to collect the data, or forget to bring them to the meeting.
- The data is always summative or formal data.
- Teachers don't know how to look at or evaluate student data.

Lack of data is a problem. When teachers don't focus on student data, they tend to focus on perceptions. We all have perceptions and some of those can be backed by data, but some of arc things we have made up based on isolated experiences.

Think about it: Have you ever felt like the class was struggling when it was really just a few students who were struggling? Or have you heard a teacher make a generalization and when you asked for some clarification, they weren't able to speak to any specifics? We have all done this. We want to be sure that we are working on real student needs, not just our best guesses.

Using student data ensures that we are working on those real problems and needs. But many traditional PLCs skip the data step, and teachers end up identifying the needs of students without backup. In the second part of this book, we will talk about an even more powerful student data collection: *empathy data*, which allows teachers to drill down even further to find student needs.

Repetition over Progress

PLCs are intended to build on learning throughout the year. Teams should be in a very different place at the end of the year from where they were at the beginning. However, many PLCs seem to spin their wheels with little change occurring. The PLC cycle is simple, but it can feel repetitive, and PLCs that don't find early success struggle to build and grow. Instead of getting better with time, these PLCs tend to wither and die. Progression is necessary for members of a PLC to stay engaged and to successfully improve student learning.

Compliance Focus

Many traditional PLCs become compliance-focused, completing tasks given to them by administrators or other leaders. Administration wants to see an increase in student achievement and they know PLCs can make that happen, so they mandate processes and tools to be completed. Then the PLCs are reduced to meeting a mandatory number of minutes each week and filling out whatever compliance paper work is assigned.

Some of these tools can be helpful in keeping teachers focused on a specific task. Yet, without buy-in and engagement from teachers, the tools remain ineffective. Sometimes these tools can even become impediments to the real work of the PLC. I have been in PLC meetings where it took almost 30 minutes to complete the compliance paperwork. These meetings are thus more focused on turning things into the administration than on helping students.

Effective Traditional PLCs

I don't want to paint a picture that for the last 20 years all traditional PLCs have been awful. There have been fantastic PLCs that have had tremendous success. I have been a member of some of these PLCs, and I have also seen other great PLCs. The traditional PLC structure, when followed correctly, can be really effective. This is the reason for the popularity of traditional PLCs: the structure *can* lead to successful instruction and student learning. At their best, traditional PLCs do the following:

- Focus on student data
- Improve student learning

- Build teacher camaraderie
- Improve school culture
- Hold teachers accountable for student achievement
- Progressively enhance teacher learning and collaboration throughout the year

There are many tools and books about improving PLCs because they can do great things when they are working. There is hope for PLCs. There is hope for your PLC. You have to believe that. Belief is the first step.

The Potential PLC

If effective PLCs are able to improve student learning and can do everything they promise, then why do we need this new Design Thinking PLC structure? Because the traditional PLC is not good enough. Bottom line: even at its very best, the traditional PLC falls short of what teacher collaboration can be and what our students need.

Not only can the best PLCs become even better, but this structure also makes creating effective PLCs easier. Design Thinking PLCs make successful collaboration simpler. Here's why. They are

- High energy
- Innovative and creative
- Experimental

What's more, they

- Promote teamwork and support over accountability
- Transform the classroom

How would you like to be in a PLC that reignites the fire that prompted you to embark on a teaching career? One that put students (not student data or achievement) first. I suspect that's the reason you bought this book. Design Thinking PLCs can do all of these things. But first, you need to learn a little bit about Design Thinking. The next chapter will give you a good foundation.

UNDERSTANDING DESIGN THINKING

Now that you know that your PLC could be better, you will want to learn how to make this happen. Before I can share with you how Design Thinking PLCs can transform your teacher collaboration experience, you have to understand what design thinking is. This chapter will help you understand design thinking and why this process works for improving PLCs.

Design thinking is a process to create better services, products, or processes. It originated with commercial product design, but it has since been used in many industries and organizations. Design thinking focuses on understanding what users need in order to create and test innovative solutions. Designers learn by testing their prototypes with real users and determining how to improve their solution. This iterative process puts action before perfection in order to involve users with the overall design.

In design thinking, the people using the design thinking process are called designers. As you embark on this process, you can now add designer to your title as teacher and educator.

Human/User-centered Process

Design thinking is a human centered process. Whoever will use the product or service is called the end-user. This end-user is valued as the most important component when developing a product or service because ultimately whatever is being created is for this user. The user's needs must be understood. In education, our students are the end-users.

Instead of looking at outcomes or numerical data, design thinking starts by trying to empathize with the user. This involves research that connects with the end-users and their experiences. To understand user-experiences, data, such as tests or surveys, are not enough. They do not explain the experience of the user. Design thinking focuses on empathy data such as observation and interviews to better connect with user experiences and then define their specific needs.

The user is not only considered at the beginning of the design thinking process but throughout the cycle. As prototype solutions are designed, users test the product or service immediately. Designers watch the user interact with the prototype and ask questions afterward. This allows the designers to change and tweak the prototype based on observing the user and collecting the user's feedback.

Iteration

Thus, design thinking is an iterative process. It differs from the focus of many organizations, which is to create long-term plans or immediately determine solutions. Instead of spending a lot of time trying to forecast an unknown, design thinking spends time trying things out, allowing us to get our hands dirty, and learn along the way. As designers learn, they make changes wherever needed. As an iterative process, design thinking is also an actionable process. Designers learn by doing, reflect on their learning, and make changes.

Focus on Innovative Solutions

Design thinking is meant to create new solutions. Most planning processes are built around what worked in the past and adapting these to the current needs. But what if what worked in the past doesn't work now, or won't work for a specific user? Design thinking allows designers to try new solutions, not just stick with the status quo.

The Design Thinking Process

Understanding User Needs

This is the empathy portion of design thinking. Before focusing on finding a solution to a problem, designers spend time understanding the needs of the user. They dive into the problem to better understand it. They take time to observe and interview users before they do anything else.

Once they have collected empathy data, designers spend time examining and discussing the data to define their user's needs. This means really thinking through and discussing the data to create a simple needs statement that becomes the focus for the design thinking process going forward.

In education, understanding the user's needs means spending time interviewing and observing students to examine their learning process. This takes the PLC deeper into the student learning process.

I once participated in a PLC as an English teacher. As we looked at some of our summative assessments, we saw that students had scored lower on analyzing the plot than they had on understanding the characters. But I know that some of my students didn't differ at all in understanding the literary devices of these standards. There could have been a thousand reasons they missed these questions, including, the structure of the questions, difficulty of the reading, and context of the reading. And these are just issues with the assessment. If they had really struggled in understanding the plot, I didn't know *why* they struggled to understand the plot. And yet, we doubled down and decided to re-teach the plot to our students in the same way we had likely failed them the first time.

Think of it this way: in design thinking we put our student *first*. Not after determining the curriculum map or calendar, not after the needs of our administrators, or the district, or even our own needs. We put our students' needs first and define them explicitly. Once we know their needs, the rest of the design thinking process allows us to actually meet their needs.

Designing Innovative Solutions

In the design thinking process, ideation is a critical stage. Ideation is a process of brainstorming multiple solutions. Once a specific user need has been identified, the design team spends time developing multiple possibilities for meeting that user's needs. The ideation process is about creatively thinking of as many solutions as possible and then systemically selecting the best solution to build into a prototype.

Often, people follow the most obvious solution, or the first one presented. It's understandable. Think of all of the time and money spent planning for and enacting a solution and the haste to solve the problem. But this is why the same solutions are recycled: there is little or no time given to creatively thinking about multiple options.

Once a creative solution is selected, in design thinking, a prototype is created. A prototype is the simplest, cheapest, and easiest-to-create embodiment of the solution. In fact, the goal of the prototype is not to be a finished product, but the most accessible version of the solution that allows users to test the solution. Instead of spending time and energy creating a polished solution that might need tweaks, prototyping allows designers to get feedback from users before getting to the final solution.

Prototyping also allows designers to design the specifics of the idea they have developed. As designers create a prototype, they can think about all of the nuances and details that will impact the user. Many of these details may not have been part of the initial idea, but are important to ensuring that the user's needs are met.

I worked with a PLC who prototyped a project where the students designed a history museum. This was the idea, but the prototype had to include a lot of details about how this would be taught to students, what would be the format or medium of the museum model, and how it would connect with the English, social studies, and technology classes. Prototyping helps designers think through the details of the design along the way.

When you start prototyping, you have to put your perfectionist persona aside. That's why prototypes are often described as ugly, fast, rapid, dirty, beta, and messy.

Too often in education, we use the tried and true or most obvious solution. In fact, *best practices* has become a common term for how to move schools forward. Some renowned school leadership scholars even believe that seeking innovation in education is dangerous because we shouldn't experiment with students and we already have answers about what works.

The truth is that education requires iteration, not replication. One way doesn't work for all students and if we had all of the answers, the education riddle would have been solved well before now. The ideation process also allows teachers to think of new and innovative ways to meet student needs.

Finding a gap in student learning doesn't matter if teachers don't know how to address the need. What usually happens is that we just teach it the same way that didn't work the first time because that is the way we know how to teach it. *Best practices* do not always connect with *how* to teach in a new way to meet student needs because they can limit teacher options and stifle their ability to grow and adapt to students. Ideating and designing prototypes allows us to creatively try new approaches and make changes to find what works for our students.

Testing Prototypes and Reflecting

In design thinking, designers always focus on meeting the user need. In testing prototypes, designers can determine how well their solution is meeting those needs and make changes accordingly. Testing can focus on specific parts of the prototype the designer wants to ensure will meet the user's needs. Does the user like the prototype? Is the prototype user-friendly? Is it meeting the intended needs? Is the prototype efficient?

Once the prototype has been tested, the design team can reflect on the data. Based on what they have learned, what should be their next steps? Again, the design thinking process is iterative, meaning you can return to any part of the process at any time. The testing data can lead a team back to collecting more empathy data, back to ideating different solutions, or back to making changes to the prototype. Eventually, this reflection can lead the design team to complete the prototype and make it a permanent implementation, though this usually doesn't happen on the first test.

While testing has been a standard in education, it has been focused principally on student knowledge and often measured through a very specific means. Testing prototypes allows teachers to measure multiple student learning needs, which includes engagement, understanding, connection, comportment, etc. Yes, we want our students to learn. But through the design thinking process, we have identified unmet needs that are impeding learning. Through prototyping and testing, we can begin to see how we can meet those needs in ways that will ultimately lead to improved learning.

3

WHY DESIGN THINKING WORKS FOR PLCs

Now that we have identified problems with traditional PLCs and shared the basic structure of design thinking, we can explore why design thinking is an excellent process to improve PLCs. The following reasons should start to convince you why you should make your PLC a Design Thinking PLC.

Creates New and Innovative Solutions

We know what we know. That is why the ideas and solutions we come up with are generally based on what we have done in the past. This is one of the reasons that the routines of school are perpetuated over decades. We teach as we were taught. When teachers come together to collaborate, it can become a session of sharing what we are already doing, not designing new and fresh ideas we have never tried before. Even when we do try something new, it is generally based on what another teacher has done that has been successful.

Most of the systems we have in place in education are all about building on past practice. But today's students are not the students of yesteryear. And just because a teaching strategy worked on one student doesn't mean it will work on another.

Design thinking helps teachers create new solutions to meet unique student needs. Its iterative process means that a solution is always being developed, tested, changed, and retested. Innovation requires change. If the past practice was working for all students, we could point to one model that would help them all be successful. We all know that that model does not exist. By using the design thinking process in collaboration, teachers can create new ways of teaching that will support the students in their classrooms.

Ensures that the Student Voice Is Heard

We all want to help students. For the most part, we think we know what is best for them. In a world where standards and outcomes are created far away from a classroom, it is easy to lose the student. Even when student data are considered in designing curriculum, it doesn't consider the actual student, just the student work. In a sense, this process reduces students to numbers and words.

Design thinking starts with the student, our end-user. We must connect with them and understand their experiences in order to design solutions that will help them succeed. The empathy portion of design thinking allows us to really understand the needs of the student and the testing portion allows us to reevaluate what students are learning and still need to learn. In many ways, this is the most revolutionary part of the design thinking. Real teaching should always address student needs. But when classrooms are set at 30 students or more, when we are focused on curriculum, when we are limited by time, it is easy to lose the student.

Fosters Teacher Creativity

Teachers are not robots. None of us signed up to be told what to do or to read a script. We have all seen education reduced to this in the name of guaranteed viable curriculum or standardization.

Most teachers want to be creative. It is exciting to create a new lesson and then see the learning happen as our instruction meets student needs. Creativity inspires and motivates both teachers and students. A creative faculty is excited to come to work every day and engage in lively discussion. A creative faculty is a true professional learning community that promotes a culture of learning within a school.

Administrators can sometimes be wary of allowing teachers to be creative because they are concerned that they will abandon all rational teaching practices. They worry that teaching will become about fun and games without any real objective. This is why design thinking is great for teacher collaboration. It focuses the creativity on student learning. Yes, teachers are coming up with new ideas and creating innovative prototypes, but they are completely focused on student needs and student learning. A creative classroom does not have to be a chaotic classroom.

Helps Teachers Define Actual Student Needs

A creative classroom can meet the needs of a diverse student body. Teachers often make assumptions about how to support students or what they need. Sometimes, we make these assumptions based on our own experiences. It is easy to forget that every student is different and the complexity of students' lives means there are a number of reasons why students are struggling. Even academic achievement data can lead to assumptions, because it only presents what the student does or does not know. Academic achievement data alone don't allow the teacher to understand why the student does not know or cannot accomplish something.

Design thinking presents an opportunity to dig deeper. Teachers are able to understand the motives behind student learning. They are able to define a specific need, based on observation and student interviews. In traditional PLCs, the focus is on **what** a student needs to learn and measuring whether they have learned it. Teachers then make plans as to how to support students if they did not learn, but those plans generally do not involve **why** the student has not learned. Design thinking allows teachers to understand student needs and define the why. This previously missing component empowers PLCs to truly support student learning in the way they were intended to.

Creates an Iterative Course of Action

Part of the PLC process is an opportunity for teachers to learn together and make changes based on student needs. However, this process often leads to small tweaks in instruction that do not create substantial change. Teachers are looking at student learning issues and trying to make changes, but the process does not provide a means to develop new strategies for success beyond planning. Incremental change is often the result of this process and is not always successful.

In the design thinking process, the ideation and prototype stages allow us to think outside the box and create new solutions for student learning. We then test these prototypes with students and collect new data. The new data allow us to find out what is working and what needs to change. We can then return to the ideation or prototype process. This process allows the possibility for sufficient and deep, even radical change.

Teachers are truly rethinking their teaching approach and trying new ways to support student learning. Constant improvement of the process leads to improved teaching and student learning over a sustained time.

Allows Teachers to Create Multiple Solutions

When we find a problem or need, we generally use the same tried-and-true solutions we have always known. This, of course, leads to repetition and doesn't often lead to success. I have been guilty of re-teaching a student in the exact same way that didn't work the first time. We are a solution-driven culture, and we focus on the fix instead of allowing time to consider all of the possibilities, thus perpetuating repetition and not supporting the creation of new and more viable solutions.

The ideation stage of design thinking allows teachers the time and space to collaboratively consider multiple solutions to student needs. They learn multiple ideation techniques in order to improve their creative thinking and they find ways to generate solutions that uniquely meet the needs of students. By learning how to generate multiple possibilities instead of jumping in and planning out a repetitive or unproved course of action, they learn how to improve their teaching and add new skill sets to their repertoire.

Focuses on Student Data

Traditional PLCs have helped teachers to focus on student data, a foundational element. Done consistently, this allows PLCs to support student learning. Unfortunately, collecting data is a missing piece of the process of ineffective PLCs.

PLC members often start with a desire to collect data, but meetings are wasted when not all team members collect them. Teachers might feel the data they are collecting are not connected to the most important things they need to accomplish every day, or they are unaware of how to collect the data. Many traditional PLCs set an expectation to collect data, but rarely discuss how to collect data it or assist other members in doing it.

In design thinking PLCs, teachers work collaboratively to decide what student empathy data need to be collected. Because design thinking designates a shared student need that all members of a PLC are working on, teachers are more likely to be engaged as they have been part of the focus of the PLC and are designing their instruction around it.

Teachers in Design Thinking PLCs also create an empathy protocol, which includes specific plans for collecting data and analyzing them as a team. Later in the testing stage, teachers also collect data on teaching and learning practices and schedule time to analyze those data by creating a prototype testing protocol. This shared process improves the participation of PLC members in the student data collection and analysis processes.

Makes PLCs Actionable

The real power of using design thinking in the PLC process is that prototyping makes the PLC an actionable process. Teachers are not just leaving with a plan; they are leaving with a prototype. As they test that prototype in class with students, they are able to return to the PLC with additional data and make changes as necessary. The PLC was set up for this work, but design thinking makes the work actionable as teachers build tangible solutions.

Builds on the Current PLC Model

Because Design Thinking PLCs are structured around the basic ideas of traditional PLCs, most schools already have an infrastructure for PLCs to meet. Adopting the Design Thinking PLC model instantly into schools reinvigorates teacher collaboration. While teachers need training and support with the new model, it does not require creating an entirely new system. Design thinking works with existing PLC teams.

Are you convinced of the power of design thinking to transform your PLC? Would you like to start a Design Thinking PLC? The next chapter will help with that.

DESIGN THINKING PLCs

Now that we've discussed the traditional PLC, the process of design thinking, and how it can improve PLCs, it's time to look at what makes up a Design Thinking PLC. This chapter is an overview of the basic structure of the process. The remaining chapters are a step-by-step guide through the process.

This overview will help you wrap your mind around the basic idea of the structure. Don't worry if you don't understand everything right now as these ideas will be explored in much greater detail in later chapters.

What Design Thinking PLCs Need

A Collaborative Team

Every PLC needs a collaborative team. The "community" part of the phrase is a dead giveaway. But even though having a collaborative team seems obvious, in the design thinking process, teams are especially important. Collaboration is the act of working together. Since design thinking involves processes like problem-solving, ideation, and prototyping, the work of the collective group is important in taking the team to new places and new ways of thinking. Iteration and change happen best with multiple minds and voices in space together.

Think about it. If you could figure out how to move forward on your own, you already would have done it. And if you were to do the work of a Design Thinking PLC on your own, you would probably come up with what you have always done. The synergy of the team is what helps us to see new possibilities and our unique perspective supports the creativity of the entire PLC.

Education is not the only industry where teams are necessary. Almost every innovative organization is fueled through creative teams. The myth of the lone inventor or entrepreneur is just that, a myth. If you peel behind the curtain of Apple, you realize it took a lot more than Steve Jobs to create and design all of those products.

If you have ever been a part of an amazing collaborative team as a teacher, you know it is fantastic. You may even be part of one now. Design thinking simply makes those teams better by giving them a platform to get creative through an iterative process.

If you are reading this with fear or concern, I get it. You might be the only one in your PLC reading this book. You might have a dysfunctional

PLC, or you might wonder if your administration will support this new way of thinking about PLCs. These are all valid concerns. The last chapter is all about how to gain support for launching a Design Thinking PLC. So, if you have a team ready to go, introduce them to this process. If not, be sure to read the last chapter.

The Spirit of Design Thinking

Once you have a team onboard, you need to be sure your team understands the spirit of design thinking. You all have to be open to finding ways to understand student perspectives and let those guide your work. A lot of teachers are nervous about listening to students. They think students will want what is easy, not what is best for their learning. But you won't be listening to student wants; you will be investigating student experiences.

Everyone has to agree that they will really try out iteration and be open to testing and experimenting. Teachers are often afraid of failure and so they resort to what they know best: the tried and true, what they have always done. Design Thinking PLCs require teachers to be vulnerable. At the same time, the team is there to support us and we are there to support the others. It is a safe place for innovation and learning. Learning requires stretching ourselves. The team must be willing to push themselves and support each other. That is the purpose and goal of a true professional learning community.

I once worked with a Design Thinking PLC that had a strong leader. This teacher already knew what she wanted to work on with her team, so she tried to use the process to get where she wanted to go. It didn't work.

The PLC was unable to make the student empathy data go in the direction that the leader wanted because the student needs were not exactly what the lead teacher had thought they were. The point of Design Thinking

PLCs is to uncover and meet the needs of the students. Teachers have to be willing to work through the process to make that happens regardless of their assumptions.

Trust the Process

Design Thinking PLCs are structured but not stringent. Some educational programs claim the need for fidelity to a process. Instead, Design Thinking PLCs require flexibility and the potential to change plans and start fresh. So, there is a process to follow, but we have a lot of freedom within the process. The important thing to remember is you cannot skip stages, meetings, or tools.

We have to follow the process. Teachers who don't use a needs statement don't have a Design Thinking PLC. You cannot have a Design Thinking PLC without collecting empathy data or without designing a prototype. The Design Thinking PLC process is designed to support teachers in innovatively meeting student needs, but it won't work if it is modified or not followed.

Have you ever tried making a recipe without a key ingredient? Or skipped a step in the baking process? If you don't follow the recipe, things don't turn out right. Design Thinking PLCs allow for plenty of improvisation within the process, but the process itself must be followed.

Follow the process. Trust the process. You got this. You are going to make a difference for your students. And you are going to have some fun along the way.

Design Thinking PLC Structure

There are a lot of moving parts within a Design Thinking PLC. The graphic below puts it all into one visual. This process is based loosely on the design thinking process created at the d.school[2] at Stanford University, but it adapts the model into a working process for PLCs.

Design Thinking PLC

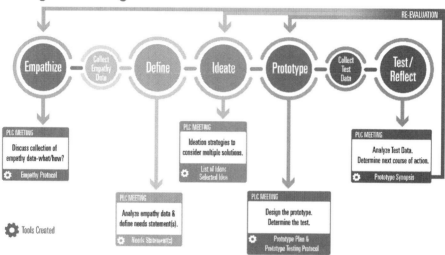

Design Thinking PLCs are broken down into categories to help you navigate through the process and connect all of the moving parts. Again, this is just to give you an overview of the process. We are going to spend a lot of time going through all of these components step by step. Here are the navigational categories:

- Design Thinking Stages (These come from the d.school design thinking model):
  - Empathize
  - Define
  - Ideate

---

2 d.school (n.d). Retrieved from https://dschool.stanford.edu/

- Prototype
- Test/Reflect
- PLC Meetings: There is a PLC meeting objective for each stage of the design thinking process.
- Classroom Action
  - Collect Empathy Data
  - Collect Test Data
- Design Tools
  - Empathy Protocol
  - Needs Statement
  - List of Ideas/Selected Solution
  - Prototype Plan
  - Prototype Testing Protocol
  - Prototype Synopsis

During the Design Thinking process, your team will enter distinct design thinking stages. You will have PLC meetings that help you through these different stages. Between meetings, you will take action in the classroom based on those meetings. You also will use tools to complete the work of each of these stages. Some of these tools will help you in completing your work in meetings and some will help you in your classroom action. Each of these categories of the Design Thinking PLC process will ultimately help you meet student needs through teaching and learning.

Along with the chapters in this book, there is a *Design Thinking PLC Playbook* that accompanies this book. The *Playbook* has graphic organizers and other supports to help you through the process. The *Playbook* is free and can be downloaded at https://www.newschoolinnovation.com/design-thinking-plcs.

Design Thinking Stages

The different stages in the design thinking process are similar, but defined with a focus on students in the Design Thinking PLC:

- Starting Point
- Understanding Student Needs
  - Collecting empathy data
  - Defining student needs
- Designing Innovative Solutions
  - Ideating solutions
  - Prototyping
- Testing and Reflecting
  - Testing prototypes
  - Reflecting on results

Starting Point

The starting point launches the Design Thinking PLC cycle. The purpose can be any of the three Ps: problem, program, or pedagogy. The PLC decides on a specific purpose they want to explore. The starting point doesn't give a direction for the Design Thinking PLC, just a starting point to launch the initial empathy data collection. Chapter 5 will help you define your starting point.

Understanding Student Needs

In order to understand the student needs around the selected starting point, teachers need to learn about the students' experiences. Chapter 6 will help you understand the importance of student voice in the design thinking process.

As PLC members collect empathy data, they can identify specific student needs that will guide the Design Thinking PLC in creating new solutions. Teachers will create an empathy protocol to determine how they will collect empathy data around the starting point. They then use this empathy protocol to collect the data, usually through student interviews and observations. Chapter 7 will guide you through the process of collecting empathy data.

The Design Thinking PLC collectively evaluates the empathy data and creates a student needs statement. This needs statement is what drives the PLC to the next stage: designing innovative solutions. You will learn how to create a student needs statement in Chapter 8.

Designing Innovative Solutions

Once the Design Thinking PLC has developed a student need, they spend time ideating multiple innovative solutions before selecting one solution to prototype. The team then spends time designing the initial prototype and determines how to test it. Chapter 9 will help your PLC develop an experimental mindset, Chapter 10 will guide you through the ideation process, and Chapter 11 will help you develop a prototype.

Testing and Reflecting

Teachers collect specific data from the prototype tests. These data will determine what works with the prototype and what needs to be improved. Your PLC will build a testing protocol for you prototype. Chapter 12 will help you learn how to test your prototype.

Once you have tested your prototype, the Design Thinking PLC collectively examines the testing data and reflects on what steps should be taken next. The PLC can choose to return to any stage in the design thinking process. Specifically, the PLC can decide to:

- Collect more student empathy data around student experiences with the prototype.
- Define new student needs.
- Ideate alternative solutions based on learnings from the initial prototype.
- Refine the prototype.
- Declare the prototype a success, adopt new practices, and enter a new design cycle.

Chapter 13 focuses on reflecting and determining next steps in the design thinking process.

PLC Collaboration Meetings

Design Thinking PLC collaboration meetings work best when they occur at least once a week, though I have seen successful PLCs meet every other week. These collaborative meetings are important because this is when collaborative work takes place between teachers. In every meeting, teachers work through one of the stages of the Design Thinking process.

A sample of the evolution of collaboration meetings is shown below. This evolution is not set in stone. Sometimes, an entire meeting is not needed to create a starting point, so it can be combined with developing the empathy protocol. Sometimes, a PLC needs a whole meeting to evaluate empathy data and define a need, but sometimes it happens quickly and the meeting can move into ideation.

A basic structure for Design Thinking PLC Collaboration Meetings is shown below:

- *Meeting 1- Starting Point*: Teachers discuss a shared issue to explore.
- *Meeting 2- Developing an Empathy Protocol*: Teachers determine what empathy data should be collected to define the student need. The PLC develops an empathy protocol to determine how data will be collected and includes a plan to bring those data to the next meeting in order to define the student need.
- *Meeting 3- Define Student Needs*: Based on the empathy data collected, teachers define one to three needs statements. These statements will serve as the foundation for the instructional work that will happen going forward.
- *Meeting 4- Ideate*: Teachers brainstorm several solutions to the needs statement. They allow themselves to be creative. After creating several solutions, teachers work together to select a solution to try out.
- *Meeting 5- Develop Prototype/Test*: Teachers start to design out the solution they have chosen and decide how they will test it in the classroom. The prototype does not need to be a holistic instructional shift of all teaching but instead a way to try something out quickly and collect data to see how it works. Teachers decide when they will test prototypes and what data they will collect to determine if the solution is meeting the student needs statements.
- *Meeting 6- Evaluate Prototype Data/ Reflection*: Teachers bring back data from the prototype and decide what is working and what needs to be changed. They can decide to return to any part of the design process. They can make changes to the prototype and try it again, or they may decide to go back to the empathy stage and collect more student data.

Classroom Action

Classroom action is the work teachers do between collaborations to collect data from students and to test solutions with students. Most classroom action is taken by teachers individually, though there are opportunities for teachers to team up with release time to observe each other's classrooms and support each other through the action process.

The classroom actions that Design Thinking PLC process focuses on include the following:

- Collecting empathy data by interviewing specific students and/or observing classroom behaviors and procedures.
- Testing prototype designs in the classroom; these are generally instructional, but can vary in design.
- Collecting testing data from prototypes.
- Observing or supporting instruction in other PLC classrooms.

Design Tools

Several design tools will support the work of your Design Thinking PLC along the way. These can be found in the Design Thinking Playbook that you can download at https://www.newschoolinnovation.com/design-thinking-plcs. Some of these tools are optional. The tools you need to complete along the Design Thinking PLC process include the following:

- Empathy Protocol
- Student Needs Statement
- List of Ideas/Selected Solution
- Prototype Plan
- Prototype Testing Protocol
- Prototype Synopsis

The Founding Patiño Staff- A Case Study

The first time I was part of a Design Thinking PLC we had not yet coined that phrase. In fact, I wasn't even aware that we had created a professional learning community, but that is exactly what we were.

When we decided to create the Patiño School of Entrepreneurship, I was able to involve my staff in a design thinking process to design the school. We read several resources to learn about what design thinking and we attended a week-long workshop at the d.school at Stanford, a program focused entirely around design thinking. We also visited schools that had implemented innovation or design thinking models.

Once we understood the basics of design thinking, we put the process into practice. We interviewed our first enrolled students to understand their needs. We tested things out. Based on some of our readings, we decided to implement a "disorientation" process during the first week of school to shake students out of the traditional learning model. We had students use design thinking to create the school mascot, motto, and logo. As we designed these processes, we were continually testing what was working and what we needed to improve.

What really made this a Design Thinking PLC was that we were consistently running through the design thinking process throughout the year. In other words, we didn't just think through the cycle one time. Rather, we returned to ideation when it was needed, built new prototypes, and collected more student empathy data. It was also a real PLC because it was about the work, not a formalized meeting schedule. We didn't even call this work PLC; we just met when we needed to collaborate to make things happen.

I am not saying that a set meeting schedule can't be a powerful support for Design Thinking PLCs. What I am saying is that the meetings cannot mandate Design Thinking PLCs. We were immersed in designing a school model that worked for our students and brought the power of entrepreneurship to life. The meetings and the structure were all about supporting that work, but we had to buy into the iterative process. We had to believe design thinking could create transformative educational opportunities for our students.

This is how Design Thinking PLCs were born. It would be years before they would take on this name and before we started to formalize the process and tools in this book, but the work of collaboration through design thinking started as we designed a new school and a new school model. It was an exciting time and I will never forget some of the collaborations we shared as educators. The same energy can be shared at any school that catches the vision of Design Thinking PLCs.

From Prototype to Product

The Design Thinking PLC structure is based on iterative testing. Just as you will be doing with your students, I worked with my own Design Thinking PLCs to identify teacher needs and prototype solutions.

It's important to note that this is more than just a mashup of design thinking and PLCs. Instead it has evolved through constant testing. After I journeyed through the design thinking process with my staff at the Patiño School of Entrepreneurship and refined the process along the way, I took the initial prototype of Design Thinking PLCs to other schools that I consult with to further test the structure. Many of the tools and processes contained in this book were designed through identified teachers' needs that we discovered from observations and interviews.

From my considerable experience with design thinking, I believe that this basic structure can transform your PLC and your classroom. I have seen it happen! Before you know it, you will see the innovation in your PLC meetings and ultimately in your classroom. In the next chapter, you will explore how to start your first Design Thinking PLC cycle.

UNDERSTANDING STUDENT NEEDS

PART 2

THE STARTING POINT

Now that you have a basic understanding of the Design Thinking PLC structure, you are ready to get started. The first question is, "Where do you start?"

When I became a teacher, I was on fire. I wanted to do everything I could to help my students and I believed in instructional planning and improvement. I actually loved being a part of any meeting that focused on improving my teaching and when my district started instituting PLCs, I was excited to have more time to collaborate with my colleagues.

I find that most teachers feel this way about teaching and learning and care deeply about students. Why else did they get into this job? Despite what some critics think, it probably wasn't for summer vacations and it certainly wasn't for the money. So then, why do PLCs get stale and stagnant when the teachers in them want to do what is best for their students?

Many PLCs lack focus. We know that PLCs are supposed to focus on student learning. There are good work books available that try to solve the focus issue by prompting teachers with questions and graphic organizers about student learning. These can help some of the time, but more often than not, they serve to support that compliance culture of filling out forms and meeting tasks instead of working toward student needs. These PLCs can get bogged down in long-term planning or surface-level sharing about the present reality. And even in answering these questions, there is a disconnect with what students really need.

One of the strengths of design thinking is that it takes PLCs through a structured cycle with a focus that still allows for flexibility, freedom, and creativity. So, once you get into the design thinking cycle, the structure can help you stay focused. The only thing the PLC needs to launch a focused design thinking cycle is a starting point.

Getting Started on the Starting Point

How does a Design Thinking PLC get started? This is a critical juncture of the Design Thinking PLC process. When you commit to a design thinking cycle, it means you will spend a lot of time, often several weeks, diving into student needs and investigating a set of solutions. You want to make sure you are heading down a path of value for students.

This is the place where many PLCs fail—right at the beginning. They don't know what to focus on. Some PLCs never get there; they don't have a focus. They just swim around in generalities. I have been in PLCs where it feels like we are wandering in the jungle and have no clue what we are doing or where we are going.

Other PLCs start somewhere because one teacher threw something out when nobody else could think of anything. These PLCs technically have a purpose, but the real purpose is just to do something to pass the time. The teachers haven't bought in because there hasn't been a shared focus or a shared concern.

Having a starting point gives your PLC a jumping off point for your design thinking journey. But remember, your work will change and be transformed through the Design Thinking PLC process. So it doesn't have to be the perfect starting point. You shouldn't spend days deciding where to start. You just need something of importance to investigate. As long as your team can bring something to the start, the process will take it from there and make it something meaningful.

The three Ps are an easy way to decide your starting point. PLCs that talk through these Ps can generally find something in common, something in which all team members are willing to invest time, investigation, and design development.

The Fourth P— Purpose

This isn't really one of the starting point Ps, but it is a P that defines what your starting point is. When you have a starting point, you develop a purpose for your PLC. This purpose will evolve into a student need, but initially having a reason why you are meeting with other teachers and going through a design thinking process will help you get excited about the work you are starting.

The best thing to do is to make a list of possible PLC topics for the three Ps listed below. Each teacher in the PLC should come to the first meeting prepared with some different ideas from each of the Ps. To make this list, you can use a graphic organizer (see https://www.newschoolinnovation.com/design-thinking-plcs).

When the PLC meets, teachers share their lists and explain each of the potential starting points. The group can create one collective list or jot down all of the starting point ideas on the board. Members shouldn't initially worry about selecting a starting point. This will happen at the end of the meeting. The initial goal is to list all potential starting points and share them with the PLC.

Problem

Of the three Ps, problem is the most common. This is also the P that often drives traditional PLCs. Teachers can bring problems they identify from their classrooms into the PLC for support through the design thinking process. A lot of things can be identified as problems: students struggling with content, issues with instructional delivery, or underwhelming student work ethic.

It is important to remember that teachers really don't understand the problems they bring to a PLC. The Design Thinking PLC is an opportunity to investigate a problem and find out why it is a problem. It is an opportunity to dig deeper. You may start with a problem, but you are going to use the first phase of the design thinking process to understand that problem and define the student need.

This is a differentiator between Design Thinking PLCs and traditional PLCs. A traditional PLC will start to work on solutions to an identified problem. A Design Thinking PLC seeks to understand the problem or issue and why the problem exists from the student perspective.

A problem could be student data from assessments or assignments that demonstrate a gap in student understanding. You don't know why that gap exists. It could involve content knowledge, study habits, an issue with instructional delivery, test performance, or home distractions. Once you have identified a starting point of a problem, the Design Thinking

PLC you will able to learn more about what the data is really telling you about student learning.

However, a problem doesn't always have to be identified through formal assessment data. Teachers may identify issues with student frustration in a particular content area, or find that work is not being turned in. Teachers are aware when something is not clicking with students. This can constitute a problem to use in starting a PLC cycle. You may not fully understand why the problem is happening or what you can do about it, but that is a perfect reason to take the problem to a Design Thinking PLC.

You can also identify a problem based on student engagement or student behavior. If you are finding that students are struggling to engage in your class or their behavior is not what you would normally expect to see, a Design Thinking PLC can help you identify why the problem exists and create new solutions.

I worked with one Design Thinking PLC that was an interdisciplinary grade-level team. They thought that their students across the grade-level were struggling with behavior expectations that had been no problem for students from previous years. As they ran through the design thinking process, this behavior starting point turned into ways they could improve their teaching. They were able to run a very successful Design Thinking PLC by starting with this student behavior problem.

Pedagogy

Anything that has to do with teaching constitutes a starting point for a Design Thinking PLC. Pedagogy is a starting point that focuses on *how* teachers will teach in the classroom. There are a number of pedagogical strategies that you may want to implement. The starting point does not have to be based on a deficit in the classroom. Teachers can decide that they want to implement new teaching strategies to improve their instructional approach. Or teachers may need to implement new pedagogical strategies based on new approaches by the school or district. If there is a new teaching strategy you want or need to implement in the classroom, a Design Thinking PLC will help you get there.

There are a number of hot new pedagogical approaches in education circles. These include project-based learning, small-group instruction, linked learning, and many others. Maybe there are some pedagogical practices that a teacher or PLC has always wanted to try. Write them down. Design Thinking PLCs give teachers a space and system to try out the things they have always wanted to but may have been afraid to. The design thinking structure supports experimentation and gives opportunities for testing things out, reflecting, and making changes. In other words, you can't fail. So don't worry about what you don't know or what might happen if things go wrong. A new pedagogical approach is a great starting point for Design Thinking PLCs.

Sometimes, a new pedagogical approach isn't the idea or desire of a teacher or PLC, but it comes from the site or district administration. Because of some of the shifts with recently adopted standards, many districts are trying to find new ways to teach. Some of these pedagogical approaches may fall in line with ones that teachers have identified as things they have always wanted to try and some of them may not.

One of the frameworks of PLCs is that they are teacher-driven, so some teachers might be hesitant to use a mandated pedagogy as a starting point in a Design Thinking PLC. However, design thinking will always lead to a *student*-driven process once you start figuring out student needs. So, you can feel free to start with a district-, site-, or teacher-driven starting point because whatever the starting point is, it is going to be transformed into a student-driven focus through the Design Thinking PLC system. If this is a practice that teachers will have to adopt anyway, why not use the power, support, and creativity of the Design Thinking PLC to put it into place?

Another great way to launch a Design Thinking PLC is to use pedagogical problems as a starting point. This combines the two Ps of problem and pedagogy to create a single starting point. Teachers can ask themselves these questions:

- What are the pedagogical or instructional practices in my classroom that are not working?
- At what times in my instruction and teaching do students struggle, lose focus, or ask questions about direction?
- What parts of my lesson planning are difficult to figure out how to teach?

These great questions will spark teachers toward identifying some of their own needs to redesign. Teachers can identify what needs to improve in their class. It might be student independent work. It could be using technology in the class, or possibly direct instruction or group work. Teachers won't need a list to choose from because, in this instance, the need will come from their own classroom.

This is also a good place for teachers to reflect on feedback they have received on places to improve in their teaching. This feedback may have come from an evaluation, another teacher, or even a student. This feedback may have been painful or frustrating at the time it was received, but the Design Thinking PLC gives teachers an opportunity to put this feedback into action.

Whether it is identified by teachers, administrators, or students, adopting a new pedagogy or changing an existing pedagogical practice is a great starting point for a Design Thinking PLC.

Program

The third P, program, is more focused on the curricular side of the teaching equation. Program starting points are focused on *what* students are learning about in the classroom. These starting points can include specific curriculum, courses, projects, assignments, or activities. Many traditional PLCs focus on this program aspect through scope and sequences, syllabi, unit plans, and other instructional planning. Design Thinking PLCs, however, are less focused on long-term planning and are more focused on using these programmatic starting points to test short-term prototypes that will inform teachers how to best implement these programs to support and benefit students.

You may have a new program that is being instituted into your department or class. If this is the case, a Design Thinking PLC is a great way to understand how to implement this program in the most effective and innovative way. Whether this is a new curriculum adoption, a new interdisciplinary project, or a new intervention program, the need to implement a new program can be a great starting point to leverage the power of the Design Thinking PLC.

You can also use the Design Thinking process to look at a program you are using. Because design thinking allows you to look deeply at a program through the lens of student needs, it is a great way to identify areas of improvement in any program currently being implemented. This can be something overarching, like your math curriculum, something more focused, like your reading intervention program; or something very specific, like a project you are running in a specific unit.

Evaluating a program might not be important to a PLC because they may have already identified a specific part of the program that they would like to change or improve. If this is the case, start with what you want to change. Remember that thinking of solutions will come later in the process, so be careful to just focus on *what* you want to change, not *how* you want to change it. The design thinking process will get you to your solutions. This will be a reminder repeated throughout the book: to be patient and trust the process. If you know what you want to change, that is enough for now.

When using a program as a starting point, it is helpful to drill down as far as you can. Remember that as you identify student needs in the PLC process you will get a lot more specific, but it still helps to identify which part of the program you are looking at. For example, your entire English curriculum is probably too much to handle. So, think about what part you want to narrowly focus on. Maybe it is the writing assignments, or more specifically narrative essays. It doesn't need to be as focused as a single lesson, but if you can identify a program component, it will be easier to identify student needs and start the design process.

Selecting a PLC Starting Point

Once teachers come to a PLC meeting with a list of possible starting points, the selection process can begin. Teachers can share their selected starting points and explain them as a master list is composed. Don't take too long with this process, just long enough to allow for all of the starting point candidates to be shared briefly.

While having a starting point is crucial, what that starting point is will be less important because it will be transformed as you identify the student needs. What the starting point is does not matter as much as ensuring that the PLC has a starting point. Teachers should not go to battle to select their favorite starting point. The goal here is to find something that the entire PLC can agree on as a good place to start the process.

A master list will also give you a number of potential starting points that the PLC can draw on later because it will be running a number of different design cycles throughout the year. Improving instruction and innovating in the classroom is an ongoing process. It may take a bit of time to create this initial master list of starting points, but it will be worth it in the long run. The PLC can also add to the list throughout the year as new things come up.

The ongoing list ensures that the current design thinking cycles are not interrupted and that other starting points still have an opportunity to be addressed. Urgency should not interrupt the design thinking process and often the work of Design Thinking PLCs will solve additional starting points. A bonus byproduct of design thinking is that when you address one student need, the solution often supports multiple other needs and issues.

For example, I worked with one teacher who wanted to increase student engagement in her classroom. In her initial student interviews, she found that one of her students needed more opportunities to engage with other students in the classroom in order to engage with the content. She prototyped some work groups. As she started to test the prototype, she found that her students also improved their content knowledge and class work they turned in, both issues she had listed as possible starting points for a design thinking cycle.

Once you have a list of starting points, the Design Thinking PLC can decide how they want to select the starting point for the next design thinking cycle. There are a number of ways to make this selection. Some PLCs decide to talk through which of the starting points is of shared importance to all the teachers. This can be an effective way to select a starting point but it can also raise a few issues. First, these conversations can take too long. A PLC should not spend more than 15 minutes selecting a starting point once you have a list of options. Remember, this is not a super important part of the design thinking process; it is just the beginning. Another issue is that PLCs can have power dynamics where some members of the group might be louder or have more influence than others have. If these aren't problems, go ahead and select a starting point through discussion.

In Chapter 10 of this book, different strategies for selecting solutions from the ideation process are shared. Any of these selection strategies can also be used to select a starting point. My favorite and one of the simplest is the voting technique. Each member of the PLC puts a star next to his/her top two starting points. There isn't any dialogue about this, just each person voting. Once all members have voted, the starting point with the most votes is selected as the one to move forward. If there is a tie, there is another vote.

Whichever technique the PLC chooses for selecting a starting point, the important thing is that the team agrees on the selection. Remember, it doesn't have to be something each teacher agrees strongly with or feels passionate about. If a teacher feels like the starting point does not apply to their classroom, remind them that it is only the beginning. Every teacher will be collecting data from their own classroom and will be identifying a student need. The starting point will be transformed by understanding student needs. What your starting point is doesn't really matter. You just need to have one.

Congratulations, you have a starting point! You are ready to embark on the Design Thinking PLC journey. You need to be ready to do things a little differently than you are used to in teacher collaboration. This is an opportunity to innovate and transform your teaching. You have your starting point. You are ready. Get going!

STUDENT VOICE

Once your PLC has a starting point, you are ready to involve the end-user. Remember that this process is all about determining a solution by looking at an issue through the user's perspective. We must become adept at understanding the student experience.

The user is always at the center of design thinking. The idea is to design something that meets the user's needs. In education, the student is always at the center. We show up for work every day because there are students who need us. Schools don't exist without teachers, but they especially don't exist without students.

In recent years, a focus on student achievement was meant to ensure that "no child is left behind." However, in focusing on test data as the measure for student success, we have lost the actual student. Each student becomes a number. Most of us don't feel great about that, even though it is our reality.

Students need a voice in their own education. Education is a service for them. How do we bring the student voice into our teaching, knowing we still need to meet the requirements of the state, and the young students we teach may not know exactly what they need or how to express it?

Design thinking has the answers. By engaging with our students to understand their learning process, we can connect with them and meet their needs in ways we haven't thought of. They are right in front of us every day, but we might not have made the necessary connections. It is time to let them speak and find ways to meet their needs.

Empathy

Empathy is critical to the design thinking process. In design thinking, an issue is explored through the experience of the student. Instead of trying to design teaching around a set curriculum or whole-class objectives, empathizing allows a teacher to first understand the needs of the student.

In the empathy stage, teachers seek to collect data to understand the student experience. Teachers start with an issue or problem they need to explore. This does not mean that they know what the exact problem is, but they know that something needs to improve. For example, a teacher may understand that a student is not performing well in a particular area, but the teacher does not know why the student is not performing well and what the student's exact needs are. The teacher has identified an issue, but they still need to collect empathy data to really define the exact need.

Once a teacher has identified a starting point to explore, they decide how they will explore this issue by collecting empathy data. The data can include student interviews, student observations, or any other data collection that allows the teacher to learn about the student experience. Traditional student performance data are different from empathy data because they focus more on the outcomes of student learning or what the student already knows. Student empathy data seek to understand the student's experience of the learning process.

Student Data Meets Student Voice

Student data are an important part of PLCs. One of the purposes of a PLC is to evaluate student learning and address identified gaps through planned intervention and re-teaching. Generally, in traditional PLCs, these student data consist of assessment data, writing assignments, homework, or other formative or summative data that evaluate what students know or don't know. These data tend to focus on *what* students need to learn, but not *why* they haven't learned it or *how* to teach it. Answering these questions requires collecting qualitative data that go beyond the initial student learning data.

When student empathy enters into this process, teachers are able to dig deeper. Through student interviews and observations, teachers can start to understand the student experience. This may uncover a number of different reasons as to how a student is engaging in their learning. Empathy can take the focus into a number of different areas including study skills, social issues, and reading shortcomings. Through interviews and observations, teachers can find out what the specific needs of the student are and how instruction can evolve to meet those needs.

We have meetings and make decisions about students without ever considering their needs. It isn't that we don't care about them, but we can get trapped into seeing our jobs as a checklist. In our focus on standards and pacing guides, the student often gets left out. When we take the time to empathize with students and really understand their experiences, you start to think about how to help them as individuals. We start to care in a deeper way.

Remember, you are embarking on a process of augmenting student data and telling the whole story. A news reporter looks up facts that might be considered comparable to our quantitative student achievement. These are important details that help us to understand what students know or don't know. But they are not the whole story.

Just as a reporter or investigator would follow up with interviews, our ability to collect student empathy data allows us to get a more complete picture of our students' needs. We start to get a sense of the rest of the story that we often miss as educators. It is not only about what we are teaching, but also about whom we are teaching.

Student Experience

I have had many conversations where a teacher has told me, "We can't just do what students want in the classroom. There will never be any learning." It is important to remember that empathy is not about giving students what they want; it is about understanding their experience to better understand their learning needs.

In the next chapter, you will learn about crafting interview questions that focus on past experiences, not on preferences or perceived solutions. We want students to tell a story. This will give us the data to understand their needs and allow you to deeply connect with them. We don't directly ask them about their needs. They don't necessarily know them. And even if they did, understanding their experiences will give us a deeper look into the information that will allow us to help them.

When students share their learning stories, we are able to connect with them on a deep level. It helps us to really connect with them. Learning about successful or failed learning experiences also gives us a window into how they learn. When students tell us the story of their learning, we can start to see what works and what doesn't work for them.

Understanding the Whole Student

When students share their experiences, we as teachers get an insight into their learning process. We see where there are gaps, not in their knowledge, but in how they learn. We also get a look into their home environments and the other things they are dealing with outside of school.

Sometimes, we want to separate school life from home life. This is not a luxury our students have. They bring the issues they face in their daily life into the classroom with them. These experiences affect their ability to focus on their learning.

If we want to really support our students in their learning, we have to better understand the distractions, issues, concerns, and needs that are capturing and holding their focus. Our ability to connect academic instruction to these needs is what makes us great teachers.

We do not teach in a vacuum. Our students are complex. We cannot ignore their complexities. We need to seek to understand so that we can truly meet their needs.

Engagement, Processing, Understanding, Styles and Successes

We teachers often talk about learning styles. The research on this is scattered, but most people agree that different learning modalities exist and some of us prefer certain modalities to others. I often hear teachers talk about this: "Me, I am a visual learner, so I try and incorporate visuals into my teaching." Teachers often identify with their own preferred learning modalities, and they tend to use those in their teaching, or they employ a "shotgun" approach instead of finding out more about the actual preferred learning modalities of their students.

We can start to understand how your current students actually get engaged with learning, how they process information, when they struggle with understanding, how they prefer to learn, and how they experience learning success.

Have you ever been frustrated by the way a teacher or professor taught a class? It didn't work for you. If only they would have printed the instructions, or had more projects, or simplified the syllabus, or allowed for more flexibility. No matter how good we are as teachers, we probably have students who feel that our instruction could be improved. They may not even have the perception to label what they would like to happen; they just know it isn't working for them right now.

If you buy into the idea that you are the master of your own learning, you need to buy into the idea that your students are in control of their learning. We are their guides. And the best way we can guide them is learning about their needs and experiences.

My Empathy Conversion- A Case Study

During my first year of teaching, I had some pretty tough classes, but I connected well with most of my students except Rodney. Rodney never engaged in class no matter what I tried to do. I caught him lying several times. He rarely completed his homework. He even got caught stealing from the cafeteria.

The most difficult thing for me was that I could never get Rodney to be honest about his learning needs. I had other students who struggled, but

I could have honest conversations with them about their learning and they were willing to make goals and work toward improvement. Rodney was always defensive and seldom willing to admit the need for improvement. This was one of our conversations.

"Rodney, I notice you are having difficulty showing effort in class."

"No, I do."

"Well, usually, you aren't paying attention. I understand if you need help or support and I want to help you, but I just need you to give your best effort."

"I do try. I pay attention. I do."

At the time, I thought that I was connecting with my students and hearing their voices. I thought that I was demonstrating empathy by asking their learning needs and making goals with them. The problem was that I wasn't finding out what their real needs were, just having surface level conversations about their efforts. Their issues were actually deeper than their effort and focus. And Rodney was the student who first taught me the importance of empathy.

I was able to demonstrate empathy for Rodney only after I learned about his real experiences. I didn't learn them through my conversations with him. Those never went anywhere because I wasn't really trying to understand him. It was another teacher who was conducting real empathy interviews, not my shallow imitations, who helped me learn about Rodney. I was in the staff room one day, talking about how I couldn't figure out how to reach Rodney. The teacher turned to me and said,

"You know he and his mom have been homeless for most of the year. Just staying with family from place to place, sometimes sleeping in their car."

I will never forget that moment. I think I stood there stunned for several seconds. Everything that had mattered to me before about Rodney's misbehavior and academic apathy suddenly seemed less important. I could understand things more through Rodney's experience. I could understand why homework wasn't that important to him or why he might try to steal food from the cafeteria.

That moment not only helped me to change the way I saw Rodney and how I tried to help him; it changed the way I thought and taught. It changed me as an educator. That is the power of empathy and understanding our students' experiences.

Our students don't wear their experiences on a nametag or notecard placed nicely on their chest. They don't walk into our classrooms and announce their experiences. They are often buried and hidden. If we don't take the time to try and understand their experiences, we will not truly be able to engage them in meaningful learning.

Empathy isn't easy. It requires a lot of effort to really connect with students and give them a voice in our classrooms. But we can get there. The next two chapters teach strategies for collecting student empathy data and defining student needs. As you invest in these practices, your PLC will really start to see improvement with your students because you will be creating solutions for their real needs. You will be meeting them where they are.

COLLECTING STUDENT EMPATHY DATA

In order to empathize with students and understand their needs, you must collect student empathy data through interviews and observations. These data will help your PLC define student needs and start designing solutions. Most teachers have never formally collected empathy data. This chapter will take you through the process of planning for and collecting student empathy data that will serve as the focal point for your Design Thinking PLC.

Developing Empathy Protocols

Your PLC will need to determine which empathy data are the best to collect to better understand your starting point issue and how to collect them. Your PLC will create an empathy protocol in a PLC meeting to determine your course of classroom action. An empathy protocol is a plan the PLC develops to outline the empathy data collection process.

Once the PLC discusses the issue they want to explore, they

- Design a method for data collection
- Decide how many students will be involved in the process
- Design initial questions for interviews or a process for observation
- Decide what kinds of students to interview (are there students with specific needs to consider?)
- Create a timeline for the data collection process
- Decide what form of data the team will bring back to the PLC for analysis and design.

Think of your protocol as your master plan for collecting data. The empathy protocol assures that your team will know specifically what data they are collecting and how to collect them. The PLC will discuss issues they have and share strategies, fielding questions along the way. In designing Design Thinking PLCs, we found that there were numerous occasions when teachers were unsure how to collect data or what data to collect. Once the empathy protocol was developed, teacher success rates with data collection improved greatly.

Usually, teachers collect data in classrooms, though Design Thinking PLCs can interview students during a PLC collaboration meeting. Be sure to design time in your lesson plan to meet with students, or find a time outside of classroom instruction if necessary. Interviews and observations will not happen if you do not intentionally plan time to make them happen.

Sample PLC Empathy Protocol:

Issue: Many students are not turning in homework.

Process: We will interview three students each to understand their needs. These interviews include two students who have not consistently turned in homework and one who has regularly turned in homework.

Possible Interview Questions:

- Share an experience when you had success completing your homework.
    - What made the experience successful?
    - How did you feel in completing your homework?
- When was a time you struggled with completing your homework?
    - Why was it difficult to complete?
    - How did you try to complete the homework?
    - What did you do when you struggled?

Teachers will use prompts to dig deeper into initial questions as needed.

Data Collection Process:

- Teachers will take notes during the student interviews that summarize the student responses.
- Teachers will conduct interviews during the week before the next PLC meeting.
- Teachers will bring notes collected during the interviews to the next PLC meeting.

A template for creating an empathy protocol is available (see https://www.newschoolinnovation.com/design-thinking-plcs).

After your PLC has created the design protocol, you will need to prepare to collect your data and get it collected. Be sure to decide with your PLC when you will have your data ready for the next step at your next PLC meeting. One of the purposes of the PLC is to ensure that team members are accountable to each other. If team members fail to collect data, your PLC will not be able to move on to the next step of defining student needs. Be sure you are accountable to the group and encourage your team members. Ask how things are going with data collection and offer to help if needed.

Individual Intervention vs. Whole-Class Instruction

When design thinking PLCs identify an issue to explore, this does not mean they will need to interview the entire class. Sometimes, PLCs will see issues in student data that highlight the needs of only a small number of students. This presents an opportunity to create a plan of intervention for small groups. In this form of a design thinking PLC, the student needs and prototype are built around a group of learners within a classroom.

Even though you will probably not interview all of your students, designing for the needs of a small number of students or even a single student can improve instruction for the entire class. Design thinking is not about creating a solution to meet everyone's needs; it is about creating a new and innovative solution to a particular problem. Design solutions can be for the whole class, even when only created by interviewing a few students.

Crafting Student Empathy Interviews

An empathy interview has a unique purpose: to understand the student's learning experience. The following tips support that focus:

- Questions must be open-ended and allow students to tell their stories.

- Questions cannot be leading or have a binary answer.
- Teachers should not try to get to a specific conclusion.
- The interview must be focused on the student's experience.

If teachers ask students directly about what they need or how to fix it, students will give their interpretation of the experience. This is not what you want. Students may not know their why—you will need to find that out through analyzing their story. Let them guide you through their learning story.

Be sure to tailor interviews to student age and understanding. Here are some pointers:

- Try to create a conversational atmosphere. Don't make things feel too formal.
- Start with some easy questions to break the ice.
- Use extremes. Asking about the best or worst experiences leads students to share stories where their needs are obvious.

Sample questions include the following:
  - *Tell me about a time in class when the lesson made a lot of sense to you and you just "got it."*
  - *Tell me about a time in class where you were really confused about something.*

- Prompt deeper dives into experience.

Sample questions include the following:
  - *How did that make you feel?*
  - *Why did you feel that way?*

- Follow the story of the student's answers. Don't be afraid to deviate from your planned questions in order to follow the needs the student is expressing.

Practice Makes Perfect

Empathy interviews require practice. In order to become a good qualitative interviewer, we must continually interview people to learn how to prompt more discussion and dig into their needs. Don't expect to be an expert the first time you interview a student. You will get better with time and learn as you work on techniques with your PLC.

There are a few proven ways to practice and improve empathy interviews as a PLC. One is to invite students to your PLC meeting. As you interview them, other teachers can listen and take notes, and after the interview, you can debrief. Sometimes, this can be a positive experience for students, but it can also be overwhelming and intimidating for some students to be interviewed by a group of teachers. One-on-one interviews can feel more casual and natural.

If you do engage in group interviews, it can be helpful to invite several students and break up your interviews. Groups of two teachers interviewing students throughout the room can make the environment feel more casual and natural.

Another way to calibrate your empathy interviews is to audio-record student interviews. You can bring it to the PLC and the group can collectively listen to the interview. The PLC can then talk about the interview techniques, what was learned, how the interviewer prompted the student, or what could have been done differently.

Your PLC may not need to practice interviews; you might just need time. The more cycles you complete in the Design Thinking PLC and the more empathy interviews you conduct, the easier it will be to conduct empathy interviews.

Keep it Conversational

When you are interviewing students, it can feel a bit awkward or overly formal. You talk to your students every day, so doing it in a programmed way might feel strange. Think about it as a conversation and realize it is an opportunity for your students to connect with their teacher.

Feel free to be transparent about the purpose of the empathy interview. I often tell students that I am trying to understand their experiences so I can improve their learning process. Many students are excited to participate in this process and share their experiences. It can be hard to get them to start talking, but once they get started, some students are hard to stop.

You don't need to announce it as a formal process. An empathy interview can take place kneeling at the desk of a student or at a back table while the class works on an assignment. Don't feel like you need to create a scientific environment to do this in.

The goal is to really connect with students and give them an opportunity to talk about their experiences.

Students are natural storytellers. If you use starters like "Tell me about a time when…" or "What was a memorable experience you had…" it alleviates their concerns about saying the right thing or having to interpret their own experiences. They are able to just tell their story.

As you ask questions about their experience, you do want to continue to dive deeper. "Tell me more …" or "Why do you say that?" allows the students to explain. The purpose of prompts is to keep students talking. In an ideal empathy interview, the student talks a lot and the teacher talks only a little. Your questions and prompts are meant to push their storytelling. Let them drive. Don't try to guide the experience too much.

Use Extremes

Another way to interview students is to use extremes. Talk about the best time and the worst time that a particular event happened.

The worst times will help you understand what was missing from their experience. Through the negative, you will be able to identify what didn't work, what they struggled with, what was challenging, and why. This will lead you to identify student needs. Often students will address these needs directly. Students love to talk about events that were painful or not fun. They tend to be able to identify fairly easily those events that were the worst.

Positive experiences help you identify needs in the same way, but now students will be telling you what their experience was like when things were working. Students will express conditions, supports, and techniques that led to success and these too are how you establish their learning needs.

Remember to avoid letting students interpret the experience or identify their needs. Focus on their experience story. What happened? Help them in sharing the timeline and history of the event and how they felt throughout it.

You can redirect them if necessary. If they start to interpret, take them back to the experience. *What happened that made you feel that way?* This will focus them back on the experience and the events that led to their feelings.

Using Observation to Collect Empathy Data

Observations can be useful for seeing how students physically engage, or respond to work and assignments. Collecting observation data can help teachers determine how to organize the classroom or a lesson, or how to create engagement among student working groups. Sometimes, observation data can be collected by the classroom teacher if the observed activity has students working independently. If the observation needs to address student activity while the teacher is teaching, another educator can be asked to observe the students.

Remember that these data should be about the students, not the teacher. Having another teacher or an administrator observe student behavior during a lesson can give teachers a new perspective.

In designing an observation protocol, teachers should consider the following:

- What they want to observe (small group instruction vs. whole class instruction vs. independent work vs. team projects)
- Which students or how many students they want to observe
- Time period for observation
- Which periods or subject matter to observe

Observers should take notes of what is happening as literally as possible and note how students are acting. It's important to keep judgment, assumptions, or interpretations about the behavior out of the notes. Teachers will analyze these notes later in their PLC groups.

Because you might be observing several different students or groups of students, it might be difficult to keep track of all of the data you collect. It can be helpful to use a graphic organizer or other data collection tool to help organize your notes. You can find an observation data collection tool at https://www.newschoolinnovation.com/design-thinking-plcs.

What to Look for in Observations

As you collect observation data, start by thinking about your starting point. You should observe student experiences that connect with your starting point issue. Try to understand what students are going through in their learning. Take notes on what the teacher is asking them to do, but then carefully observe student behavior. Do they talk to another student? Do they seem to focus? When are they distracted? Write all of these observations down.

It is appropriate in an observation to ask some follow-up questions of students if you are trying to better understand their thinking experience. This should not become an interview or take the place of your actual observation, but can be useful.

You should not ask students what you already know but instead ask why they are doing certain things, or what their understanding of the learning expectations are. Keep questions to a minimum to support observation, not replace it. If you need to ask more questions, set up an interview instead.

Some quick follow-up questions might include the following:

- What are you working on?
- Why are you doing (student behavior)?
- What are you learning from this activity?
- How does (activity) help your learning?

Once you have collected student empathy data, you are ready to reconnect with your PLC and start to analyze the data to define student needs. Be sure to take your data with you to the next PLC meeting to ensure your team can collectively create quality needs statements based on your data collection.

DEFINING STUDENT NEEDS

Now that you have connected with students through observations and interviews and collected some significant data, it is time to make sense of it and turn it in to an actionable needs statement. This is an important part of the Design Thinking PLC because it ensures that the empathy work you have done is more than anecdotal check-ins with your students.

It is great to connect with your students, but in order for you to move forward to really using the empathy data to support their learning, you need to define student needs. The traditional PLC focused on student problems, what students didn't know or understand. Focusing on student needs will allow you to understand why those problems exist and help you determine how to address them. Once you have effectively created student needs statements, you have a real objective that can drive the solutions you will design through the rest of the design thinking process.

Sharing Empathy Data

Your Design Thinking PLC provides an important space for you to share data. When you share your data, it allows you to process what you have learned. It also enables your colleagues to provide perspectives you might not have seen on your own.

Discuss Your Findings

As your dig through the data, share what you learned. Important quotes from students, or notes you took during your observations are appropriate to repeat verbatim. Consider sharing any of the following:

- Which ideas or comments from students were repeated?
- Which comments stood out to you as significant?
- When did you really feel you connected with the students?
- What were your significant observations?
- What were your aha moments? What was said or done that caused these moments?

Be sure that you can back up anything you say with actual data. It can be easy to start to sum up your findings with your own analysis but avoid this. Stay with the actual data. You will have opportunities later in this collaboration to collectively analyze the data. First, you must plainly describe what the data show.

Explain your process and context

As your share your data with your PLC, be sure to explain what you were teaching, what led up to the empathy data collection, why you chose certain students to interview, and any other background information that will help the team understand and make sense of the data.

As Design Thinking PLCs work together regularly, these contexts start becoming familiar to the team. Understanding your classroom context allows the PLC to weigh in with meaningful suggestions and feedback. PLCs that never really understand classroom context generally do not move beyond surface collaboration. In order to really be able to learn from each other, the team must have a sense of what is being taught and how it is taught.

Additionally, strong PLCs learn so much together that they naturally start to develop more shared contexts that drive their collaborative work. As PLC members learn from each other, their classrooms start to look more alike. This is a good thing because it demonstrates adoption of successful practices.

Tell Your Story

When you share the data, it shouldn't feel like a scientific report. Tell the story about your data in a way that connects with the other teachers in your PLC. Think about the best novels you have ever read. They use action and dialogue to advance the plot. When you share your data like a story, it ensures that you will not spend too much time with your own analysis and it makes it easier for the PLC to understand and connect to the data.

Telling your data story also ensures that each PLC member can quickly share data in a memorable way. Here's a quick example of a data story:

As I asked Gina why she feels like she struggles with the reading assignments, she paused for a while and looked down. When she looked back up, she said, "Sometimes I read what we are supposed to, but it doesn't make sense, like I didn't understand it. I try to go back and read again, but then our time is up and we have to move on. And the next part is even harder because I didn't understand what happened before."

These stories will have common connection points that will make the data analysis easier for the PLC. It will also help the PLC feel the empathy necessary to create meaningful student needs statements in the next step of the process.

Identify Student Needs

Before you can create a needs statement, you need to extract student needs from your empathy data. If you conducted interviews, chances are your students actually expressed these needs to you explicitly. This may have happened when you prompted deeper responses or asked *why*.

For example, when a teacher interviewed Jorge, he shared a negative experience about working in groups and he explained, "Well, John just went off on his own and did the work and told me to do my part."

The teacher asked, "How did that make you feel?" and Jorge said, "Well I was mad because I thought we were supposed to work together. I didn't know how to do it and I thought John would help me."

Based on this, you know that this student has the need to work collaboratively with another student during group work or to feel supported when working in groups or with a partner.

You will want to write down each student need you find in the data. There are a number of ways to do this. You can write them down on separate sticky notes. Or you can use the Needs and Insights tool in the Design Thinking PLC Playbook (https://www.newschoolinnovation. com/design-thinking-plcs).

If you collected data from observations, you may need to make some inferences about your observations to record student needs. Chances are a student didn't directly tell you their need in an experience, but you can make some assumptions based on their actions. For example, if a student had their hand raised and they were never called on, and then you observe them disengage from the instruction and put their head down, you might state a need like, "the student needs to be heard, or addressed, or have questions addressed."

This is not an exact science, but if you can be in the vicinity of what students need based on your empathy data, it will lead you to creating relevant and important needs statements.

Be sure to connect with the members of your PLC about the different needs that you identify. Look for needs that are shared or needs that you may not have identified in your research but those you think may be valid for students in your class. Feel free to talk about this through the process.

Collecting Teacher Insights

Insights are a little trickier to identify than needs because they are not explicitly stated. Insights are the *why* behind a student need, or a reason for the need. Usually, a teacher will need to think about things that were said in a student interview or seen in observations and make inferences as the reason behind the need. These are your insights.

Insights have to be connected to a student need. As you start to think through why a student was feeling a certain way or expressed a specific need, think about what need you can connect it to.

Insights contain a student's perspective and understanding of the world. Two students might share a need for individual support, but they could have completely different insights connected to this need. One student's need might be a social need for validation from the teacher that gives them the confidence to move forward. Another student's need might be an academic need to have assignment instructions explicitly given to help them process the learning objective and assignment expectations. Both of these insights are connected to the same student need, but they express different reasons behind the needs.

In the example of Jorge, the teacher identified several times when Jorge expressed frustration about not knowing what to do in the group. As the teacher asked further questions, Jorge shared that he didn't like not participating in the group assignment because the teacher would think he was lazy or the students would think he wasn't smart. The teacher had an insight that Jorge's need to feel supported while working in groups was tied to his social need to demonstrate competency.

As you identify insights, you can work together with other teachers. As you share the story of your empathy data, sometimes other teachers will have meaningful perspectives or propose insights you may not have thought of on your own. Make this a collective process. Avoid taking individual ownership of a need, insight, or needs statement.

Creating Student Needs Statements

Once you have identified needs and insights, you are ready to create a student needs statement. The needs statement connects the identified student needs with your teacher insights into a single statement, which becomes the basis for your PLC designing solutions going forward.

Your PLC has now collectively gathered several student needs and insights. Instead of deciding which are best to make into needs statements, your team should create several needs statements. Be sure to pick the needs and insights you think are most important or those that could make the most impact if you met these needs.

Needs Statement Template

This template will help you to create your student needs statement. If your statement is based on the interview of one student, use the student's name to personalize the needs statement.

_____ needs a way to _____ so that,
(Student's name)   (student's need(s))

_____.
(reason for student's need or way that student can benefit from having their need met)

Sample Student Needs Statements

- Students need a way to connect to the readings because they struggle to focus and understand the content until they can make the reading meaningful to them.
- Students need a way to understand and have confidence in their math lessons before the end of class so that they are able to practice homework problems without fear and doubt.
- Chris needs a way to connect with peers in his group outside of the classroom because his unfamiliarity and shyness are creating a lack of confidence about sharing his ideas in the group.
- Group A needs a way to check in with the teacher before the end of class so they can articulate and process assignment expectations because they struggle to process information given vocally to the whole class.

Once you have written several needs statements, you can decide which to pursue for your Design Thinking PLC. You might find that some of the statements have things in common and can be combined into a single needs statement. For example, in the example in the last section, two students have the same need but different insights. You could create a needs statement with the single need that includes both insights.

You also may see needs statements that other teachers have created that resonate with the needs of your students. Be open to selecting those statements. The Design Thinking PLC works best with a needs statement that everyone can connect to so be open to multiple alternatives.

Ultimately, you will probably select only one needs statement. Sometimes you can pursue more than one statement if the statements have things in common. Generally, though, the more focused the needs statement, the easier it is to design strong solutions, so simplify it as much as you can.

Remember that even though you are selecting only one or a few needs statements, your designed solutions will benefit multiple students. Sometimes PLCs stall here trying to find the perfect needs statement. If you have a needs statement that aligns with your original purpose and really empathizes with real students, you can move your PLC forward to the next stages of the design thinking process.

Your North Star

Think of your student needs statement as your North Star for the Design Thinking PLC. Just as travelers would use the North Star to navigate their journey, your PLC will use this needs statement to guide the design thinking process.

Your original purpose is no longer important. This was a way to get your PLC to a student needs statement. It is no longer about why you and your team started the process; everything is now focused on finding new and creative ways to meet the needs of your students. You need to continually ask yourself throughout if your ideas and prototypes meet the needs statements that you have created.

In the next chapters of the book, you will begin to prototype solutions to these student needs. Never get so lost in the prototype that you forget the need that the prototype is working to support.

DESIGNING NEW SOLUTIONS

PART 3

CREATING A CULTURE OF EXPERIMENTATION

Once your PLC has identified student needs, you are ready to create innovative solutions. Experimentation is important in every stage of design thinking, but especially in the designing innovative solutions stage. This is where you ideate and prototype. This is the part of the process where you have to be open to going out on a limb with new ideas.

This is also the phase of the process where I see teachers revert to what they know. In order to find truly new ways to help your students and meet the needs you have identified, you have to be willing to step outside of your comfort zone and push your creativity.

Growth Mindset

Doing new things is hard. What we've always done—that's easy. We know how to do that. We are comfortable doing that. But the new thing—that's scary. What if it goes wrong? What if we mess up?

We all have a fear of failure and incompetence. It feels good to be good at our jobs, to know what we're doing. Trying something new can leave us panicking.

To start the designing solutions phase of the Design Thinking PLC, we need to be ready to take on a growth mindset. Carol Dweck differentiated a growth mindset from a fixed mindset in her book, *Mindset: The New Psychology of Success*[3]. Instead of being content with what we already know and how we have always done things, we need to admit we don't know everything and be ready to learn.

Stretch to Learn

Recently, I had an interesting conversation with Cole, my 15-year-old son. He was explaining to me why he should be moved out of his honors English class. I will share with you his argument in his own words.

Cole: "I have to work really hard just to get a B, and really, really hard to get an A. If I could go into the regular English class, I could just show up and get an A. It's not my fault —I'm just not in the right class."

Have you heard similar arguments from your students? Of course, I explained to him that he had just made an excellent argument for why he is in the perfect class for his learning. I worked hard not to use the term *zone of proximal development* because I didn't want to lose him. I explained

---

3 Dweck, C. S. (2006). *Mindset: The new psychology of success*. New York, NY. Random House.

to him that learning requires us to stretch. Walking into a classroom and getting an A is not learning. It means you can already do the work and know the content. Learning requires a level of discomfort.

Whether this is your first-year teaching, or your twentieth, you have developed a level of expertise. There are things you are good at doing. These are areas of comfort for you.

As you enter ideation, it will be easy to focus on solutions you already use in the classroom. These are the tools already in your tool belt. They might be the right tool for certain student needs, but for others, they are missing the mark.

Just because a screw driver feels comfortable in your hand doesn't mean you can use it to drive a nail into a wall. Be open to new solutions. This process may force you to head to the hardware store and purchase some new tools, but then you will own them. You will expand your teaching skills repertoire.

Collective Goal

Once your PLC is willing to buy in to the design thinking process, you have a collective goal. You have already designed a student needs statement. This is what is driving your PLC through the process. Always keep this student need in your mind. It will force a growth mindset as you and your team constantly consider alternatives to meeting that specific need.

Since our society is solutions-based, it is easy to focus on the first solution that comes into our heads. We want results and a quick fix to every problem. Instead, give your PLC some time with this student need. Think about how you could fill it in multiple ways. Think of it as a great puzzle with multiple solutions, and where the most inventive solution wins.

If you can think of your collective goal as designing different opportunities for student learning, your mindset will be in the right place to ideate and prototype. If you move through these processes quickly and don't consider multiple perspectives, the process won't really transform you as a teacher and consequently it won't transform your students. Your PLC will be spinning its wheels in the same ways you've experienced before.

Think of all of your students. They are each so unique. They need you to take on this growth mindset and be open to multiple solutions in order to meet their unique needs. If you can enter this design stage with the faces of every one of your students in mind, it will allow you to connect to a deeper creativity within you. It will allow you to meet student needs in ways you never have before.

Moonshots

Most of us see change as something incremental. You might try a different brand of laundry soap and feel like you have made a big shift in your life. Design thinking pushes for change that is more substantial. Incremental change doesn't require this kind of a process. As you get ready to ideate, you need to go big or go home.

Perhaps you have heard the term moonshot. This refers to the goal the United States had in the 1960s to land a man on the moon. Early on, the goal seemed outlandish. Impossible. But that mindset changed as the entire nation watched Neil Armstrong walk on the moon.

What is your teaching moonshot? The goal that is just so out there it is almost crazy, but you believe you could actually get there. Creating moonshots ensures we move beyond incremental change to something much more substantial.

Best-selling business author Jim Collins created the term *Big Hairy Audacious Goal*[4] to describe a goal that is really out there, but just possible enough that it can drive you to excellence.

As your PLC gets ready to enter the designing solutions phase, think about taking a few moonshots. This mindset will ensure that you are developing solutions that are just crazy enough to make a difference for your students.

Be inspirational! Change the world! Because when you find a way to reach a student who was struggling, that is exactly what you do as a teacher. If you can start to consider a moonshot, you are going to put yourself in a position to design those types of learning experiences for students.

What's the Worst that Can Happen?

What if I try a crazy idea and it blows up in my face? Or if it doesn't work?

Remember this is an iterative process. You should actually expect problems along the way. The problems are what lead to better solutions. When your prototype doesn't work, you get to see what needs to change and fix it. You get to dig deeper into student learning needs to create better learning solutions.

Keeping the iterative nature of this process in mind can help you as you enter into the ideation process. You have nothing to lose. You can be creative and inventive because you are not designing a final solution, you are designing a prototype. It is another step along the path to better teaching and learning.

---

4   Collins, J. (2001). *Good to Great*. New York, NY. HarperCollins Inc.

A Supportive, Progressive PLC

Learn from Each Other

Remember, you are not embarking on this journey alone. Having a learning community to support you is one of the best parts of this process. However, you have to be open to this learning. Teachers can use group collaboration to show what they know or establish their expertise.

Instead, recognize you are entering a new kind of professional development. You haven't done this kind of work before, so you have to think like a beginner. You are going to need to learn from those around you.

Think of this as a great opportunity. You are learning about ideating and prototyping and you have colleagues whom you can learn from along the way.

Push Creativity

One principle often affiliated with PLCs is accountability. Teachers are supposed to hold each other accountable within a high functioning traditional PLC.

Accountability is definitely part of Design Thinking PLCs, but it looks quite different. You need to hold each other accountable for creativity. Your willingness to think outside of the box will increase when others are challenging you to be more creative. Strong Design Thinking PLCs foster creativity.

As you embark upon this creative phase of design thinking, be ready to cheer on the creative efforts of your colleagues. As we will discuss in the next chapter, we tend to self-edit our own thoughts. If you encourage creativity, you will support the creative potential of your PLC.

Support

A Design Thinking PLC that supports innovation is transformative. It can give you the courage to try something completely new and help you avoid abandoning everything when things don't go perfectly.

The first six teachers I hired at the Patiño School of Entrepreneurship were constantly being pushed to develop a new system of project-based learning designed around entrepreneurship. Even though I was pushing them as their principal, they were tentative. These were expert teachers who were used to being successful in the classroom. It was hard for them to be vulnerable and try new things.

I soon learned that it was only through the support of their Design Thinking PLC that they had the courage to step into the abyss and create completely new strategies, curriculum, and pedagogy. When it came from me in a top-down fashion, it was never very successful. Once they trusted each other enough, their ideation process became creative and they started to design truly innovative prototypes that had a real impact in the classroom.

Will I Be Perceived as a Rebel?

I have talked with teachers who have told me, "I don't want any trouble. I don't want to be perceived as a rebel or malcontent."

I struggle to relate to them because I think we need some more rebels in our schools, but fair enough. You might not want your administration wondering what in the world you are doing in your classroom. I often tell teachers that design thinking is an improvement process. It pushes you to be better at your job.

The last chapter of this book goes into greater detail about communication with your administration and colleagues in order to garner support for Design Thinking PLCs. But if you have concerns right now about your ability to really get creative to make this happen, let's review what you are doing.

Standards-based Innovation

You haven't gone rogue. You are teaching the standards. You are focused on student learning. You are simply trying out new ways to teach. You can still use your given curriculum. Even if you are in a strict curricular structure with daily lesson mapping, Design Thinking PLCs allow you to explore innovative means to meet student needs within the system.

Remember, this is innovation focused on *how* you are teaching more than *what* you are teaching. The question of how to teach has largely gone unanswered in education circles and been left to teachers and PLCs. Through the design thinking process, you are answering that question in the best way possible.

Connect to Student Needs

You are meeting legitimately identified student needs. Who would ever fault you for that? This is not experimentation done without a purpose or based on the whims of a teacher. This is student-centered experimentation to support student learning.

You are doing everything you can to support students. If anything, this process will make you better at it, not worse. Because you are willing to get creative and experimental, you will be able to improve student learning and student achievement. Trust the process.

Tell Your Story

If you are worried about perceptions, remember that you will be able to share what you are doing and why. Armed with information about how you have collected student data that led you to try new ways to meet student needs, you will be able to explain why you have designed experimental prototypes.

You have the power to explain your reasoning. So don't let fear hold you back. You need to be innovative and your students need your creativity. Be bold!

The Experimental Teacher- A Case Study

I will never forget the day I walked into a teacher's classroom and he was finally going for experimental teaching. He was teaching a lesson that was incorporating social media and I could see he was attempting big things.

I could also see that he was failing miserably. The lesson was one of the worst I had ever seen. There were failed connections, students were unsure of his expectations for their work, and they really didn't understand what they were learning. The lesson lacked the necessary structure to get students to the ambitious outcomes it was seeking.

The teacher came to me at lunch. His head was down. He said something to the effect of "Well, that was awful." I immediately praised him for trying new things. This is what I had been waiting for, and I told him I wanted to see more of it. I agreed that it been somewhat disastrous, but I pointed out all of the things I thought the lesson was trying to accomplish and that I thought it could accomplish with some tweaks. He was surprised by my reaction, but it immediately changed his demeanor. He started to talk excitedly about what he hoped could happen in his classroom. I didn't need to offer much feedback as he quickly ran through all of the things he would change to improve the lesson.

After a few days, I went back into his classroom. He was teaching a lesson that was building on the efforts from the atrocity I had seen just a few days earlier. The students were excited and engaged in creating a real social media campaign for social impact. There was energy and learning in the room. Student teams were busy planning with each other. When I talked to students, they were able to express what they were doing and why they were doing it. They understood their learning from not only the context of the classroom, but also how it was going to be meaningful for them in life. It was one of the best lessons I have ever seen.

I tell you this story to help you understand that this teacher could not have gotten to the amazing lesson without first surviving the train wreck. He also never would have gotten there if he feared the train wreck.

He had great ideas and had designed an inventive prototype. The prototype was a failure, but the failed prototype led to the lesson the students needed. Had he been afraid of what could happen, he never would have shared the ideas or designed the prototype that led to engaged student learning.

Get Experimental Now!

You have to go for it now. Don't be timid. Don't be afraid. Share big ideas. Design bold prototypes. Realize that the only way to greatness is through great risk. But realize that the beauty of schools is that students will come back the next day and you get to try again.

With a growth mindset in place, you are ready to design innovative solutions. The next chapters will teach you how to ideate and build prototypes. But don't forget to be bold. You've got this!

10

IDEATION STRATEGIES

The next phase of Design Thinking PLCs is to ideate multiple solutions for the needs statement(s) your PLC has developed. This is an important stage in the design thinking process and you must fight any temptation to skip it or run through it quickly.

Ideation takes time. I have worked with PLCs who have claimed to have gone through the ideation stage, but they have not used any specific strategies or created a list of potential ideas. The time and focus spent at this stage will be seen in the prototype and the success of your ultimate solution.

What Is Ideation?

Ideation refers to creating multiple possible outcomes, solutions, or choices. Brainstorming is one ideation technique. The focus of ideation is generally on problem solving. Ideation techniques are developed structures that can help teachers to generate more ideas. Many of the ideation techniques that support student learning use the power of teams to promote and build multiple ideas, while also using voting structures to select solutions.

Divergent and Convergent Thinking

The skill of ideation is based on the concepts of divergent and convergent thinking. *Divergent thinking* involves looking at a problem from multiple perspectives and possibilities and developing as many solutions as possible[5]. Divergent thinking is not a time for dismissing ideas. It is a generative process, and all ideas are accepted. As the chemist Linus Pauling once said, "The best way to have good ideas is to have a lot of ideas and throw the bad ones away." In divergent thinking, you allow yourself to have bad ideas.

We tend to self-filter. We often don't want to make a comment in a large group unless it comes across as smart or funny. When we have an idea, we often push it away as not good enough. We also tend to critically examine the ideas of others, focusing on why a solution won't work or isn't good. This focus on the negative doesn't allow us to build and develop ideas. Divergent thinking helps us break out of that pattern of killing our own creativity.

Convergent thinking is the process of coming to a single answer. We focus a lot on convergent thinking in education. While there are times when

---

5   Brown, T. (2009). *Change by design: How design thinking transforms organizations and inspires innovation.* New York, NY: HarperBusiness.

convergent thinking is important, it does not always allow us to develop the most innovative solutions to problems. We often select the first and most obvious solution and then spend excessive time planning it out and finding a way to make it come to fruition. We can be more successful in finding the best solutions through convergent thinking if we have first practiced divergent thinking.

The amount of time spent developing bad ideas is astonishing. When we problem solve, we need more divergent thinking before we get to convergent thinking. But we also can't spend forever brainstorming ideas that aren't possible or never go anywhere. Ideation marries the processes of divergent and convergent thinking, allowing time to get wild with ideas, but later focusing on which ideas are best to pursue to create a real solution.

Good convergent thinking leverages good divergent thinking. When you have a number of solutions, you can develop strong processes to pick the best solutions. If you don't have a good convergent process, it can waste the efforts of the divergent process. This chapter will introduce you to multiple strategies that promote both good divergent and good convergent thinking.

Ideation in PLCs

The group dynamics of PLCs make ideation especially important. We often negate creative ideas in groups because we don't want to sound stupid, so we avoid ideas that might be too off the wall. This form of self-filtering promotes mediocrity and the status quo over innovation. Design Thinking PLCs allow a safe place to think outside of the box and get creative. Your team will support this creativity and you will give yourself license to try out new ideas. You will converge in your thinking later in this stage, so there is no risk. The ideas you throw out are not selected solutions, just possibilities.

Group dynamics also often promote compromise. Because we want things to run smoothly and we want to get things done, we often don't wait to select a best solution, just a solution the group can agree on and get us moving forward. If there is someone in the group really sold on an idea and is pushing it forward with a strong will, it can be easy to bring that solution forward as a path of least resistance.

But don't our students deserve better? Shouldn't we find best solutions that uniquely meet their needs instead of settling for first solutions, easy solutions, or compromised solutions?

Including a strong ideation process as a phase in your Design Thinking PLC ensures that you will create multiple possible solutions and select possibilities that give your students unique learning experiences that will meet their needs.

Creating a List of Ideas

Whichever ideation techniques and strategies you select, it is important that you create a list of ideas. Your list can be a crazy mind-map on chart paper or an organized spreadsheet with ideas grouped by category. What your list looks like will depend on your ideation strategy. The most important thing is to have a list.

Creating a list of ideas ensures that you have really done your due diligence as a PLC to create multiple possible solutions. Quantity leads to quality. There are no rules about how many ideas you need to have, but it can sometimes help the ideation process to have goals. Deciding you want to come up with 50 possible solutions can really push your creativity during the ideation process.

In addition to having a list for selecting a best idea to prototype, it is also resourceful to keep your ideation list. Remember that the design thinking process is fluid. After testing prototypes, you might want to return to your ideas if the prototype doesn't work.

Having a strong list will enable you to make a best selection. Remember as you start with ideation strategies that this is the divergent part of the ideation process. Get as many ideas as possible. Go for moonshots. Don't be afraid of getting a little bit crazy.

If you would like a way to collect and keep your ideas in one place, see the List of Ideas worksheet found at https://www.newschoolinnovation. com/design-thinking-plcs.

Ideation Strategies

The likelihood of your PLC ideating effectively is increased if you have some group-accepted strategies to guide you through this process. I have listed three strategies below, but there are hundreds to thousands of ideation strategies. I suggest you try several out and see which work for your group. Also, don't be afraid to switch it up and see if different strategies will help you find different ways to generate ideas. Even if one works well for your group, different ideation strategies might help your team generate different kinds of ideas.

Group Ideation

Several ideation processes exist. Some of my favorites involve group ideation. In group ideation, teams of three to five people are given a certain amount of time to develop possible solutions for a problem or needs statement. A needs statement is our blueprint to solve the real problem. It's good to limit the time to 15 minutes or less because the work time will be intense and high energy. I encourage groups to stand for this exercise. Each member of the group writes their ideas on sticky notes and posts them on a board as the ideas occur to them. They also say the idea out loud as they place it on the board. This is better than having one person writing ideas because it allows everyone to participate. Each person can build on the ideas presented or have new ones. The point of the session is not to explain the idea in detail, just to write it and post it. Crazy ideas are welcome as they often lead to some really creative possibilities. The goal is to come up with as many ideas as possible.

After the idea generation session, the team can start to think through the ideas posted. As they read through them, they can ask questions about what certain ideas mean. They can also start to group ideas that are similar, that work together, or that complement each other in some way. This is where groups start to really discuss and understand the possible solutions in further detail. This is a processing time and serves as a transition between the divergent and convergent thinking stages.

Finally, teams vote for the solution they want to pursue. There are number of ways to do this described further on.

A variation on this process is to have team members spend the first 10 minutes writing their ideas on their own silently and then posting them all at the same time. While this lacks the high energy of the group ideation and doesn't allow for building on other ideas, it does support more introverted team members.

Mind-mapping

Mind-mapping is an ideation strategy with its own slew of different processes. There are entire books and software devoted to mind-mapping strategies. Here, I'll share a fairly simple version of mind-mapping, but your PLC can get more complex if they want to.

Mind-mapping involves mapping out our thinking into a visual. You may have done brain-storming or thought bubbles like the one below. This is a version of mind-mapping.

Write down as many thoughts as you can think of. Get them on the page. Make connections with lines as you think of them. You can also create new ideas and connect them as you look at your map. Don't worry about having a super-organized map. You can outline it later if you want to. The goal is to just get your ideas out.

The strength of mind-mapping is that you allow your brain space to throw out ideas. You can make connections with lines and often these connections are what spark new ideas. You are allowing previous ideas and thoughts to give you new ideas to build on. This is one of the ways our brains work, building connections. Below is an example of a mind-map I created for this book (sorry for the sloppy handwriting):

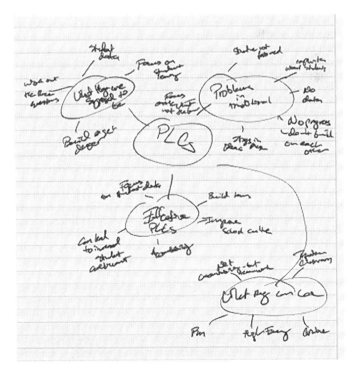

You can create singular mind-maps and then connect them as a group, finding common ideas and deciding how ideas connect. You can also create a group mind-map on a white board as another form of group ideation.

If you want to use a paper mind-map that you can keep with the rest of your Design Thinking PLC materials, see https://www.newschoolinnovation.com/design-thinking-plcs.

Decide as a group how you want to mind-map. There are many options-your PLC just needs to determine what your process will be this time. Your final map can serve as your idea list.

Structured Incubation

I love the ideation techniques that happen in a PLC. These are high-energy sessions that create team unity and excitement. Creativity is fun! But most ideation doesn't happen in a *Eureka*! moment. When we have the great idea come to us, it is usually because we have been thinking about a problem or a need for a long time.

Structured incubation does not happen in a session like the other forms of ideation. In structured incubation, the PLC team chooses a few categories for ideation around the needs statement. Your group then sets up shared documents and gives the group a timeline to add ideas to the document.

The benefit of structured incubation is that it gives your PLC time. You allow yourselves to think about ideas and add to the list over a defined period.

Structured incubation goes wrong though when nothing happens. You have a busy life with a lot going on. A lot of times, PLCs come back to their next meeting with very little ideation progress and mostly blank documents.

Here is where the structured part of the incubation comes into play. Your PLC needs to set accountability goals. These might include the following:

- Have five new ideas by half-way through the week.
- Send an email by Thursday (or any day) describing your ideas up until this point.
- Have a goal for a number of ideas by the end of the week.
- Schedule a five-minute call or meeting to share idea progress so far.

Structured incubation can be a great way for your PLC to find the time to come up with some great possible solutions. Just be sure you create a plan to ensure that this strategy will lead to a quality list of ideas.

Selecting Solutions

Once you have a list of possible solutions, it is time for your team to start the convergent process of picking a solution to prototype. You are in a better place now to do this because you have worked collaboratively to create many possible solutions; having a strong convergent process will ensure you select the best possible solution(s) to prototype.

Grouping

Once you have a list of ideas, your PLC can start to group your ideas by category. Not only will this allow your team to organize your thinking, it is also an opportunity for the PLC to process the ideas that have been generated. During the grouping process, team members can ask questions about different ideas and give explanations.

When you are grouping, be sure to note when categories are different solutions that are around the same area and when ideas can actually be connected into a single solution. This is important.

I really like using sticky notes in the grouping process. If you used group ideation as your ideation strategy, then you already have your ideas on sticky notes. If not, I think it helps to transfer your list to these notes. This will allow you to move ideas around as your form groups and then give these groups a category name.

You want to give sufficient time to grouping, but don't let yourself get stuck doing this forever. Ten minutes is usually plenty of time. Any more than 30 minutes is too long. Remember, you will have more time to design these solutions out further in the prototyping phase, so just use the grouping as a way to get to the next step.

Impact/Feasibility Chart[6]

This is not a step you have to take in your ideation process, but if your team has the time it can be a valuable part of the convergent process.

Creating a impact/feasibility chart involves taking the top ideas your team has talked about in the grouping process. The idea is pretty simple. You take a sticky note with the solution on it and decide where it fits on the impact/feasibility continuum. *Impact* refers to what degree the idea could support and fulfill the student needs statement. *Feasibility* refers to how likely or easy the solution will be to create.

6   Gray, D., Brown, S. & Macanufo, J. 2010. Gamestorming – A playbook for innovators, rulebreakers and changemakers. Sebastopol, CA: O'Reilly Media, Inc. http://gamestorming.com/impact-effort-matrix-2/

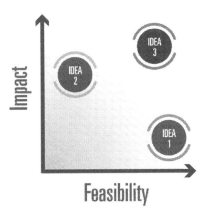

In the chart above, Idea 1 has low impact but high feasibility, Idea 2 has low feasibility but high impact, and Idea 3 has both high impact and high feasibility.

Most ideas tend to be high feasibility but low impact (the kinds of ideas we have already done a lot in schools) or high impact but low feasibility (the kinds of ideas with an unlimited budget). The goal is to find ideas that are both high feasibility and high impact.

As you chart ideas, you may start to see some ideas in a different light. An idea that seemed great before may seem less so when charted and some ideas may seem better once they have been charted high on both axes. This will accelerate your voting process. Sometimes, voting is not even needed as one solution becomes obvious through the charting.

Another opportunity that presents itself through using the impact/feasibility chart is the chance to modify ideas. You might have a moonshot of an idea that really isn't feasible. This is a point in the ideation process where your PLC team could think about how that idea could be modified to be more feasible. A crazy idea could become workable with a few tweaks and a feasible idea could become more impactful with a few

changes. You can find a free impact/feasibility chart at https://www.
newschoolinnovation.com/design-thinking-plcs.

Voting

Now that you have grouped your ideas into categories and have poten-
tially charted their impact and feasibility, it is time to select which idea(s)
to prototype. Generally, one solution is all you will select. Sometimes
PLCs decide to prototype a few solutions that different teachers test out,
but usually one solution will suffice, especially when you are just starting
out. Sticking to one solution will simplify your process.

Most traditional PLCs use discussion to decide how to proceed. The
problem with this technique is that it doesn't always allow for the best
decisions. Often, the person with the most influence in the group will
push an agenda, or a compromise will be reached to appease everyone.
Our students deserve more than this.

In the ideation process, every solution belongs to everyone. This has
been a collaborative process and ideas have been built on by others. Don't
campaign for an idea you hold dear. You can pick your idea, but respect
everyone else's right to do the same.

Voting respects everyone's voice. It does not need to be a public process.
I suggest the following strategies:

- No talking during the voting process. This will stop campaigning
  and persuading.
- Each person votes for the two ideas they think best meet the
  needs statement and should be prototyped. This allows for more
  votes and a broader version of solutions.
- Vote by putting a star or sticker on the sticky note with the solutions you would like to prototype.

- The idea with the most votes wins.
- If there is a tie, revote with only the final two solutions. Each person votes once. Same rules.

Once you have a solution selected to prototype, you are ready to move on. Finishing a true ideation stage means that your PLC has explored many options and selected one you all feel confident in prototyping. This stage takes time, but you are in a stronger place now to move forward then you would be if you had not explored many options. You also have ideas you can return to later if necessary.

PROTOTYPING

Now that you have a selected solution, your team is ready to create a prototype to test the solution out and improve it.

The pedagogical focus of most schooling tends to be one right answer for each question. As a professor, I often find students asking, "What are you looking for on this assignment?" In other words, what is the right answer? This is what a system focused on standardized tests promotes, an idea that every question has one answer. Many teachers also promote this idea in their classes. Feedback is largely focused not on an analysis of work and thought processes, but on a marking of right or wrong on the answer. College is often no better where general education courses are often measured by little more than rote memorization and tests based on facts from textbooks and lectures.

Because of this one-right-way ideology, teaching generally comes under the same microscope. Terms like *guaranteed-viable curriculum* and *pacing guides* suggest that teaching needs to look the same in every classroom.

Yet, we all know that most problems do not have only one answer. Even the ones that do are often arrived at through a process of trial and error. A renewed value placed on critical thinking and problem solving in both the professional and education worlds proves the importance of a skill such as prototyping.

Different student needs will require different pedagogical approaches. One of the problems with the current education system is that instruction is reproduced to a classroom full of students year after year in the same manner. When students don't learn something, the class often moves on, or it is retaught to them in an intervention format, but the intervention is often taught in the same way as the initial instruction.

Prototyping is the process of building an imperfect solution. The purpose of the prototype is to test it, find its flaws, and improve it. Instead of focusing on the "right" way to teach, teachers create something that meets student needs, test it out, seek feedback, and make changes. This is how good problem solving happens. Most scientists and mathematicians generate models they can disprove in order to find ways to a proof or a solution.

In the world of design, the idea of rapid prototyping allows designers to build a quick archaic prototype to test a product. This process often involves cardboard and duct tape and looks more like a third-grade art project than a design for a professional product. Instead of wasting time and money building the wrong product, prototyping allows designers to test new ideas and products before they are built. It allows them to get to the right product with testing, instead of trying to get to the right product without help.

Classrooms and Prototyping

Classrooms are a dream prototyping environment. Every day, we get to work with a group of students who are ready to test your prototype. We can observe them testing our prototype. You can seek their feedback. And regardless of their experience, they will show up again tomorrow to test any changes we make.

Entrepreneurs would love to have access to this kind of a test market. Some people might cringe when they hear a classroom referred to in this way, and teaching as experimentation is not comfortable for everyone. Student learning is important and some would argue students should not be treated as guinea pigs or lab rats. However, you have identified a student need that is not being met by the current system. You need to try something new.

Experimentation is how we improve learning. Really, all teaching should be a prototype. Meaning that we test what works and what doesn't and make it better. Prototype doesn't mean we are putting out an inferior lesson, it means we are putting out the best instruction we can think of to meet a specific student need and then determining what we can do better.

If we keep offering students what we always have, we will always get the same results. When we prototype, we will have failures, but we will learn from them along the way and become better instructors. So, don't think of prototyping as putting an inferior product in front of students. Think of it as continuous improvement. Teachers who prototype end every school year in a very different place than they started and so do their students.

Kinds of Prototypes

In the world of product design, prototypes are often constructed using very basic materials. A prototype for a children's toothbrush was constructed using a tooth brush head, popsicle sticks, and duct tape. Software designers often create paper prototypes, which are simply wireframe drawings of each screen on a piece of paper. They have testers touch the paper as though it were a computer or smartphone screen, and are then presented different pieces of paper for the next screen of choice.

The point of the prototype is to be simple. You should not spend a lot of time or money creating a prototype. Though teaching prototypes differ from these other prototypes, the same principles apply. You want your prototype to be the quickest way to learn what needs to be improved and what you can move forward with.

I think teachers can overdo it sometimes without testing things first. They put a lot of time into trying to create a perfect lesson. I am not saying teachers should always be winging it. What I am saying is that a prototype helps your lesson designs. As we teach a prototype, we quickly get a sense for what is working. We can respond to student reactions instead of trying to guess what they will be. Prototyping allows us to plan tomorrow's lesson while we teach today.

Lessons vs. Tools vs. Supports

What does an instructional prototype look like? It is hard to define because it can be a thousand different things. While the next section will give some specific examples, instructional prototypes can generally be divided into three categories: lessons, supports, and tools.

Lessons are complete instructional packages. They are built to teach a specific skill or meet a learning objective. Lessons are the default for teachers in determining how to teach because teachers use lessons every day with students. Prototyping lessons can include creating an entire lesson as a prototype, prototyping the way we design and deliver lessons, or prototyping a specific part or technique of lesson delivery.

Units are a collective set of lessons. While a unit or project may be our overall solution, it is good to break prototypes down into the lesson format so that we have an opportunity to test our teaching quickly and get feedback for our longer-term unit. Lessons are a great instructional solution for prototyping but it isn't the only prototyping possibility.

Tools are generally something physical that support student learning. These include graphic organizers, manipulatives, and computer programs. Tools differ from lessons in that they are replicable and can be used in many learning experiences instead of in a singular learning experience. Tools can be used across lessons and help students to understand and process learning opportunities.

Supports are replicable like tools, but they tend to include strategies, processes, and people instead of physical items. These supports help students perform in learning experiences. Supports often help students overcome a specific learning shortcoming or difficulty.

Your solution ideas will often determine in large part what your prototype will look like. But remember, your prototype will be a modified version of this solution. So your prototype tool could be a hand-drawn graphic organizer that you photocopy and learn what you need to before designing a beautiful graphic organizer on the computer.

Designing your Prototype

After the ideation process, what we really have is an idea of a solution. While our PLC may have discussed quickly what this solution looks like, one of the advantages of designing our prototype is that we will be able to think through what that idea actually looks like in practice including key details.

Your entire PLC should be part of designing the prototype. This is where a singular idea becomes a team solution.

As you design your prototype think through these questions:

- How are we going to meet the student needs?
- What are the specific parts of the prototype that will introduce new learning techniques or opportunities?
- How will students engage with, or interact with the prototype?
- What parts of student learning are we testing?

All these questions will help you to design your prototype. Remember that your prototype is a bare-bones strategy to test your solution with your students. Some complete solutions will require extra funding, gathering new curriculum, or other extra work. At this point, don't worry about those things. Think about how you can create your prototype in a cost-effective, time-efficient manner.

If your prototype tests well and you learn how to best implement the solution, you can then build a more complete solution that may include budgeting and strategic planning across multiple classrooms. For now, your PLC just needs the easiest way to test the idea.

Design Strategies

You might wonder how you go about actually designing your prototype with your PLC. One strategy is to simply sit down and start to write out the prototype with your team. However, many PLCs feel it is beneficial to use other kinds of more creative design strategies that really unleash the creative brainpower of the team. There are a number of ways for your PLC to design your prototype. Some of these include the following:

- Creating an outline of all of the components of the prototype.
- Drawing a picture or diagram of the prototype process.
- Creating a story of the prototype from the student perspective.
- Creating a physical design of the prototype.
- Building a lesson plan in a template.
- Role-playing the instruction with your PLC.
- Creating a video of the instruction or a video that explains the prototype.

Be sure that when you leave the meeting, everyone is aware of what the prototype is so that it will actually be tested in the classroom. Creating the prototype plan explained at the end of this chapter will help you to do this.

Individual Intervention vs. Whole-Class Instruction

Based on your solution, your prototype might be something you create for the entire class, or it might be something that applies to a specific group of students. This is something you may have already thought of as you identified student needs and ideated. But it is when you design your prototype that you will really need to determine how your solution applies to instructional groups and where your prototype best fits.

Remember that the needs of a small number of students or even a single student can improve instruction for the entire class. Design thinking is not about creating a solution to meet everyone's needs; it is about creating a new and innovative solution to a particular problem. Even though your problem and need are specific, design solutions can be for the whole class.

Some prototypes will obviously fit into a small group scenario. Other prototypes are actually intentionally designed to be used one on one with students. Go ahead and move forward with prototypes for the selected student groups, but there may be other solutions where you are unsure of the scope. Yes, they were designed for the needs of a certain student, but the benefits of the prototype might be able to affect a number of students.

If you are unsure about the scope of your prototype, my recommendation is to introduce the prototype to the entire class. See what happens. Remember that this is a prototype. You will learn as you go. If you see that the scope is too large, you can dial it back and move to smaller student groups.

By introducing the prototype to the entire class, you will be able to determine if the solution is beneficial to most students. You may also be able to identify student groups you had not considered who can benefit from the prototype, or who might benefit from a prototype modification. The only way you can learn these things is by trying them out. Some of the following prototype examples might help you design yours.

Prototype Examples

PLC 1 wanted to prototype a solution to communicate more effectively with parents. Their actual solution was a website. To prototype the website, the PLC decided to create a weekly email newsletter that had a form where parents could respond with feedback. This allowed teachers to test the interactions with parents and learn how the parents responded before putting in the time and resources to build out the entire website.

PLC 2 was prototyping for a solution that broke students into differentiated level "stations" for small group instruction and specialized independent work. Instead of doing this in the whole class, the prototype was built for one small group. The teacher had the group working on independent assignments from the rest of the class, and then the teacher broke away when the whole class was working independently to work with this small group. Another teacher came in during the small group instruction to observe and take notes. The PLC was able to study and learn from the notes and the teacher was able to have an outside observation of her teaching and the student engagement.

PLC 3 was prototyping a project-based learning solution involving team project roles. Each teacher tried out different roles in groups for the same project. Teachers created a shared tool to takes notes while they observed students working in teams throughout the project. They also created a survey for students to evaluate how well the roles worked within the groups. This allowed the PLC to evaluate the notes and surveys and determine which group roles worked best and how they could revise the experience for better group/project outcomes.

PLC 4 wanted to prototype a solution for elementary school teachers to switch students for subject-matter interventions. They decided to create different prototypes on different dates for math, reading, science and social studies. On Monday, they sent students who needed support in math to one room, and moved students who didn't need help to the other rooms. On Tuesday, they did the same thing for reading, Wednesday for science, and Thursday for social studies. This allowed the teachers to test the instructional intervention prototype without worrying about the logistics of the rotation. If they found out the instruction worked and this was a model they wanted to adopt completely, they could design a more comprehensive rotation model. But if the prototype didn't demonstrate an effective subject-matter intervention, they wouldn't have put in all of the effort to build the rotation model and communicate with administration and parents. The prototype let them see if it was worth the effort.

Prototype Plan

Once you have determined what kind of prototype you will create, your PLC will want to create a prototype plan. The prototype plan is simply an outline of what your prototype will be. The prototype plan allows you to have a blueprint as you build your prototype, helps your PLC stay on the same page, and provides a document you can share with administrators and other teaches showing what you will be trying to accomplish instructionally in your classroom.

Sample Prototype Plan:

Prototype: Parent email newsletter

Possible Final Product: Website

Purpose: Increase and improve parent contact and collaboration.

Student Need: Students need a way to directly communicate teacher expectations to their parents so they can receive support in the home and not feel frustrated when they forget to talk with parents.

Process:

- Newsletter template will be designed by PLC at next week's meeting.
- Newsletters will be sent via email to parents each Monday morning outlining plans for the week.
- Newsletters will be sent for one month.
- Each week a different teacher from the PLC will send out the newsletter.

Prototype testing (to be further outlined in the testing protocol):

- Parent survey
- Student improvement in turning in assignments/participating in activities
- Teacher discussion

A template for the prototype plan can is available at https://www.new-schoolinnovation.com/design-thinking-plcs.

Creating prototypes is fun and important. Make sure your PLC is clear on what the prototype is and how it will be implemented in the classroom. Additionally, your team will also want to be clear on how the prototype will be tested. Now that you have created a prototype, you are ready to determine how to test it. The next chapter will help you collect data from your prototype.

TESTING SOLUTIONS AND REFLECTING

PART 4

TESTING PROTOTYPES

Now that you have a prototype, you are ready to test it. One of the principles of prototyping is creating something fast to find out what works, what doesn't work, and then quickly make the prototype better.

When you decide to create a test for your prototype, remember that different components of the learning process can be tested. Really, what you will test depends on your student needs statement. If your student needs statement is focused on engagement, you need to be sure that your test examines how well students engage with your prototype. If your student needs statement is focused on student-to-student connections, your prototype should test these interactions and collect data on the quality of them. The point of creating a student needs statement is to identify the part of the learning process that is missing or unmet for students. Your test needs to help you explore this gap and how well your prototype is supporting the need.

Sometimes, when we use the word *test*, teachers immediately start thinking about traditional quizzes or standardized testing. I once walked into a classroom where the teacher told me she was testing the prototype. The students were taking an actual quiz to test their content knowledge immediately after the teacher had implemented the teaching prototype in the classroom. This might be an appropriate way to test a prototype if the purpose of the prototype was focused on students gaining content knowledge, although it would not be the only way to test for this.

When I delved deeper with this teacher through an empathy interview and talked through what the purpose of her prototype was, she shared that the student needs statement was focused on student processing and the need for students to have time to process the expectation of the learning activity and connect with the teacher to share their understanding of the learning objective.

Once we talked through the purpose of the prototype, we made a list of prototype tests that could be more appropriate:

- A student survey that asks the students about the learning objective.
- The teacher quickly asks the student what they are working on.
- The teacher observes the student working and takes notes on their understanding of the assignment.
- The teacher reviews student work and takes notes on the student understanding. The teacher can follow up with student understanding about the assignment the next day.

Ultimately, we decided to design a tool that allowed the teacher to take notes on student understanding during the next class as she tested the prototype again. This graphic organizer allowed her to see how well each of the students she was working with understood the learning objectives.

The purpose of this prototype was to increase student understanding of the assignment. These tests all focus specifically on how well the students understood the assignment. A quiz on content knowledge looks at how well the student learned the content, not how well they understood the assignment. Being able to understand the assignment should help students better learn the content, but there could be other learning factors. And we still need to test their assignment understanding first. Prototype testing ensures that we focus on each identified student need in order to improve the learning process.

I find that most student needs statements are focused on the learning process, not content knowledge. In fact, by fixing the learning problems and supporting the learning needs of students, the content knowledge does increase. Again, this means shifting the focus from *what* students are learning to *how* they are learning. It is imperative that this emphasis on the learning process is maintained through the testing of the prototype.

Also remember when you are testing a prototype, you are not just testing *if* the prototype works. You are also testing the following:

- How it works
- How it doesn't work
- How well it works
- What parts work, what parts don't
- What data the prototype gives you
- What other issues or needs the prototype unveils
- What changes you can make to instruction to further meet student needs

Sometimes, teachers get so excited about implementing the prototype that they forget to collect test data on the prototype. Remember that the purpose of the prototype is just that: to collect data to bring back to the PLC on specific needs that the prototype is intended to meet. Too often though, teachers complete the prototype and share anecdotal observations about how the prototype went. Not only does this kind of data collection lack detail, it also doesn't give us anything concrete to take back to our PLC to evaluate the prototype. This leads to storytelling and doesn't allow us to move on to reflection and decision making. We have to collect real student data.

Collecting Student Data

Just as your PLC collected specific student data in the needs phase, you will need to collect actual data from your prototype test. The new data will vary based on your student needs statement, the kind of prototype you have developed, and the area of student learning you are testing.

Observations

Observations are a great data collection tool for many prototypes, but be sure your observations are planned and intentional. You don't want to sum up the prototype experience based on your memory or by observing from afar. If you are observing specific students, be sure to take notes on your observation of each student. If you are observing groups or the class as a whole, you want to be sure you take notes about what is happening with the group overall, as well as with individual students.

I highly recommend designing an observation tool. This can be as simple as a box for each student or even just a part of the page for each student to help you organize your notes. A tool ensures that you observe the entire student group you are supposed to. Even if your tool is literal notes where you share something about each student you observe, it is better than not having any kind of tool. If your whole PLC uses the same observational tool, it will also make the data analysis process easier for your PLC.

Student Activity Data

If your prototype is something the students are doing or creating, either out of a lesson, with a tool, or with supports, the student product can be useful data for your PLC. You may not need to collect an entire class's data, but you will want data from a few students.

Evaluating student activity data in a PLC can help the PLC determine how well the students understand the prototype, if the prototype is having the desired effect, and what is working or could be improved with the prototype.

If you decide to look at student activity data, be sure to determine with your PLC how much data you will bring to your meeting and decide on a process for evaluating it. What will you look for? Be sure to connect back to the student need and don't get bogged down in other details that don't pertain like grammar or handwriting.

Surveys/Interviews

Surveys and interviews a quick kind of empathy data you can collect to understand the student experience in interacting with the prototype. Interviews do not need to be formal and can include a few questions you ask of certain students during the prototype. Be sure to record student responses.

You can also develop a survey that students take after completing the prototype. This will not give you open responses like you would collect in an interview, but surveys can give you a quick understanding of large-scale student perception of a prototype. If you decide to do surveys and have student access to the Internet, a site like Survey Monkey makes it very easy to create your survey and have the data readily available for your PLC.

Student Evaluations

If you would like more formal student feedback on a prototype, you can have your students' complete evaluations. Student evaluations are good data to collect when you have a large prototype and you want to deeply understand the student experience. Evaluations also tend to work better with older students, though you can create a simple form for elementary student evaluations.

Student evaluations should center on the identified student needs. Give students enough time to complete evaluations, or allow them to complete them as part of the prototype assignment.

Evaluations may require more time for your PLC to analyze them, so plan accordingly. I have found student evaluations to be strong data to analyze when your prototype is a large-scale project.

Creating a Prototype Testing Protocol

Just as you created a protocol to collect empathy data, this protocol will help you remember what you are testing and ensure that all PLC team members collect the agreed upon data and bring it for analysis to the next PLC meeting. A testing protocol is nothing more than a description of what the prototype will test, how it will be tested, what data each teacher needs to collect and how, and what data will be brought to the next PLC meeting. A sample testing protocol is shown below:

Sample Prototype Testing Protocol:

Prototype: Group project evaluating battles of the Civil War

Test: Understand group member engagement

Data Collection Process:

- Teachers will take notes while observing each group members participation and engagement. These notes will be taken on a tool the PLC has created (see below).
- Students will complete a survey about engagement during the project (see below).
- Teachers will collect student projects highlighting the contribution of each group role.
- Teachers will bring five of these to the PLC reflection meeting.

PLC Reflection Meeting:

Teachers will bring the following:

- Observation notes
- Student surveys
- Five group role graphic organizers

The PLC will analyze the data to determine effectiveness of the prototype to improve student engagement.

Testing Data:

Observation Tool
- Teachers will use a graphic organizer with a box for each group to separate observations of each of the student groups.

Student Survey
- Teachers will create the survey together and post digitally.
- Students will take the survey immediately following the final project.
- Survey data will be analyzed via Survey Monkey by the PLC.

You can use the prototype testing protocol template at https://www. newschoolinnovation.com/design-thinking-plcs. Once you have tested your prototype and collected data, you are ready to analyze your data with your PLC. Your data will allow you to determine the next steps in the design thinking process.

REFLECTING AND MOVING FORWARD

Once you have tested the prototype, your PLC needs to reconvene and analyze the results. This gives the team an opportunity to determine what worked, what didn't, what needs to change, and what it should do next. In this meeting, you will be able to analyze your data, evaluate the prototype, reflect on learnings, and plan next steps.

Evaluating the Prototype Data

Your PLC team should have a sense of what they are looking for in the data. If your prototype was focused on student engagement, the PLC should discuss how engaged the data shows the students were with the prototype. If the prototype was focused on student feedback, discuss how well the prototype allowed students to give feedback and what the quality of the student feedback was.

Be sure to take a deep dive into the data. As your PLC talks through the findings, try to evaluate how well the prototype worked. Take notes about what didn't work or what could have been done differently. This is not an exact science. Your team will need to draw on all of your expertise and teaching experience to really make judgments on the prototype's effectiveness.

As you evaluate with your team, get into the details of what worked and did not work with the prototype.

Creating a Prototype Synopsis

Designers tend to create a report that shares the strengths and weaknesses of the prototype. Having this report helps the design team determine how to move forward. It also provides a paper trail of data to describe the evolution of the prototype.

A template for creating a prototype synopsis can be found at https://www.newschoolinnovation.com/design-thinking-plcs. This is a basic way to fill in a form and create a record that should be useful to your PLC. You don't need a long drawn-out report, just a basic visual that gives your team an overview of how the prototype performed during testing.

What Happens When the Prototype Goes Wrong?

Of course, we want our prototype to work. We have put time and effort into creating the idea and design. We have to be sure we are honest about what the legitimate results of our test are. The whole reason we take time to test a prototype is to be sure we make changes or even abandon things that are not going to work for our students.

Be sure you are ready for the possibility that the prototype might not be the best way to meet your students' needs. If things don't work out, be ready to walk away and try something new. That doesn't make the prototype a failure; it means you have found something that needs to shift or something that won't work. As Thomas Edison said, "I have not failed. I just found 10,000 ways that won't work."

When I started the Patiño School of Entrepreneurship, an important component of the new program (or at least I thought it was) was a flex period. This period was meant to give students the opportunity to work on projects from other classes as well as on individualized online courses like foreign language and P.E. We had created this because of an identified student need to have flexibility, autonomy, and opportunity to work on group projects.

The flex period was a disaster at the beginning. We collected data and reassessed, making changes along the way. While the flex period improved, it was never a success. As we tested other prototypes throughout the school, we found that these identified student needs were being met more successfully by other parts of our program. They didn't need the flex period. It wasn't helping, it was creating problems.

At some point, I had to evaluate the purpose of the prototype. When I realized we had created better ways to support student autonomy, flexibility, and team projects, I knew we had to discontinue the flex period. That was okay. We had developed prototypes and even though I philosophically liked this one a lot, we learned about what not to do in terms of scheduling, and we had other prototypes that had worked.

Sometimes, you have to tweak the prototype. Sometimes you just need to head back to the drawing board.

What's Next?

Very rarely will you leave your first reflection meeting after testing a prototype thinking you have accomplished everything and the prototype is perfect. There will almost always need to be improvements and changes. The beauty of the Design Thinking PLC process is that you have several options for next steps after you have tested your prototype. And based on the results of your tests, you can decide as a PLC which is the right next step for you.

To Empathize, to Ideate, or to Prototype?

If you look at the Design Thinking PLC process diagram, you will see there are arrows after the reflection meeting titled re-evaluation. These arrows point back to the empathize, ideate, and prototype phases of design thinking. When your prototype isn't perfect, these are the phases you can return to in order to change or improve your prototype. Which phase you choose to return to will depend in large part by the decisions your PLC makes in the reflection meeting.

Design Thinking PLC

When to Tweak the Prototype

If a lot of things about the prototype worked, but you found a few things that could be improved, your PLC will likely return to the prototyping phase. This means there is nothing more to do than changing the prototype based on what you learned in the test and trying it out again. The length of time you will need for prototype redesign depends on how much you need to change, but generally, this only requires one or two PLC meetings. You also can reuse your testing protocol with only a few tweaks, so you don't have to reinvent the wheel. If the prototype was close, make adjustments and try again. Don't feel like you need to spend too much time here.

When to Ideate Again

When your testing shows that the prototype isn't working and it can't be fixed by simply redesigning or making changes, you will want to return to the ideation phase. You may not need to enter into a new ideation session, as you still should have your list of ideas from the last ideation phase. Your PLC can review this list and discuss whether any of the ideas already presented are worthy of prototyping. If some of these ideas feel strong, you can vote again and select one of these ideas to prototype.

Your PLC may also decide to have a new ideation session. Sometimes opening up to new ideas gets your PLC reinvigorated after a failed prototype. Your team has also learned a lot through the prototype that may add to new ideas.

When you re-enter the ideation phase, your team can decide to complete or skip any steps to the process they would like. It is really up to the team. Once you have selected another solution to prototype, you will return to the prototype phase and then the testing phase.

When to Empathize with Students

If your team decides it would like to gather additional student empathy data, it doesn't necessarily mean you have decided to start over. Sometimes, you may want to understand the student experience with the prototype. You can conduct empathy interviews or additional observations that will give you data to improve the prototype. In this case, your team will gather the empathy data and then return to the prototype phase to make changes. You won't need to revisit the define or ideate phases because you are using the empathy data to inform your work on the prototype.

Your PLC team may also decide that your prototype data has shown you that students have different needs than you envisioned, or that the student need you selected wasn't really the root issue. In this case, your team will return to the empathy stage to ask questions based on your prototype test that will lead you to define new student needs statements, ideate new solutions, and create new prototypes. If you revisit this path, your initial prototype has not been a waste. Instead, it has led you to a deeper needs statement and solution than your team would have been able to find without it.

Remember that the design thinking process is always a learning process. Your team is developing and becoming better teachers along the way. Sometimes, this takes more time or more cycles through the design thinking process than you would expect. This just means you are getting better. If you didn't work through this process, you would just be offering the same instruction that students have always received. This is a way to meet the needs that hadn't been met. It is worth it. Keep at it. Don't give up.

Are we There Yet?

This cycle of improvement can feel never-ending. While it is true you can always find things about your teaching you would like to improve, at some point your prototype will be ready to become an accepted practice. This doesn't mean you will never make changes to it, but it is now a usable instructional strategy you can count on.

Once you are ready to move forward from a prototype to a final product, your PLC can decide what final alterations need to be made. Some prototypes won't need much. You may decide to make some changes to a tool or write down the final accepted process. Your prototype may just need to be seen as a permanent practice to move forward.

Other prototypes will need larger changes to become a final product. These may include software purchases or new curriculum or texts. Some prototypes are merely testing out a larger change before investing additional time or money. If this is the kind of prototype your PLC used, it is time to decide how to move to permanency.

Your PLC will need to plan how to move forward. This process differs for every prototype. You may have to share your plan with parents or administrators. This may require some strategic planning or connecting with site administration or district resources. Each prototype differs in how it will lead to a final product or process.

Scaling

Once your prototype becomes a permanent fixture in the classrooms of your PLC team, you will have developed a best practice. Impacting the learning of your students is an outstanding thing, but this innovation doesn't need to be restricted to your own classroom. Chances are that you have created something that could support the needs of many more students. Scaling does not need to be part of your Design Thinking PLC process, but it can be.

You probably aren't in the position to simply make your new PLC innovation into a required practice throughout your school or district, but you can share it. There are many ways to scale. This is how innovation moves from small silos and islands to impact students more broadly. Some scaling opportunities include the following:

- Sharing your innovation in the staff room
- Presenting at a staff meeting
- Connecting with another PLC and sharing your process and new practice
- Presenting at a conference
- Writing a blog post or article
- Inviting administrators to see the innovation in your classroom

However you decide to scale, recognize that your development as a teacher is important to your field. Students everywhere need better teaching and learning opportunities. This book is in fact a way to scale the innovation we created in a Design Thinking PLC at one school site years ago. If it helps one PLC to improve their practice, we have scaled beyond our initial core. Scaling is work, but it is worth it.

Your Next Design Thinking PLC Cycle

Wow. You made it! Your PLC has gone through an entire design thinking cycle and created something amazing for your students. Don't stop now! This is just the beginning. Now you know the process. Your PLC has been transformed. You can't go back. You can now continue this process over and over, revisiting multiple cycles and improving student learning along the way.

The more you practice the Design Thinking PLC structure, the easier it will get. Your team will become expert empathy interviewers, strong student needs statement creators, innovative ideators, painstaking prototype designers, and radical reflectors. Each cycle will lead you to a new starting point and on to a new and exciting adventure.

Can you even remember those dull and drab PLC meetings? They will become a thing of the past as your team works to become innovative educators. You are now implementing the same process that startups, inventors, and product designers are using around the world. It's about time our students had access to this kind of thinking and teaching. They deserve it. They deserve you— you at your best. This process empowers you to develop the creativity and ingenuity that has always been inside of you.

The only thing left to do is to get others on your team. You cannot run a PLC without team members, and even if you get your PLC moving, you'll want the other PLCs in your school to get on board as well. The next chapter will help you work to establish your Design Thinking PLC and create Design Thinking PLCs throughout your school and district.

MAKE DESIGN THINKING PLCs
A REALITY AT YOUR SITE

If you have made it this far in the book, you have probably converted to the ideas of Design Thinking PLCs. You can see the advantages of using the design thinking process and what this could mean for your students. You are ready to get creative and start defining student needs, ideating, and prototyping. If it were up to you, you would already be fully engaged in your own Design Thinking PLC.

But PLCs are a team sport. This is not a process you can start by yourself. As the C in PLC indicates, you need a community. You are going to need at least your PLC team to be on board. And because PLCs are a school structure, you have probably been thinking about your school administrators as you read this book. How will they react to this PLC structure?

These are all important thoughts and questions. In order for Design Thinking PLCs to be more than just wishful thinking, you need to address these concerns. This chapter focuses on how you can make Design Thinking PLCs a reality at your site.

Be an Evangelist

Whether you like it and even though this will probably push you out of your comfort zone, you will need to be the one to make this happen at your school. You read the book; you are now the expert in the room. Change always starts in a single place. You will need to be the change.

This doesn't mean you need to dust off your trusty soap box, put it in the middle of your school, and start barking through a megaphone about the benefits of Design Thinking PLCs. That probably doesn't sound like a very exciting strategy for you and it wouldn't be very effective. But you can share your thoughts and ideas. You can share this book with others. You can tell other teachers what you want to build.

You might think that it will never work at your site. Believe it or not, schools make changes every day based on the ideas and actions of teachers. Many teachers don't think that they can affect change in their school beyond the walls of their own classroom. Yet, when teachers have ideas and work to improve schools, other teachers and administrators often responds in a positive manner.

You don't have to change every classroom; just share your thoughts in meetings and in the staff room. Tell others why you think design thinking could help improve teacher collaboration. It can come up naturally in conversation, when you discuss a problem in someone's classroom.

"What if we tried prototyping a new solution? I have heard about a teacher collaboration process that could fix that."

If you are able to start using the Design Thinking PLC within your own collaboration team and you start to have success, your school will notice. Teachers will start to ask what you are doing differently. All you need to do is share the good news. That's it. Just share what you're doing.

Use Your Current Context

We created Design Thinking PLCs to fit within the current context of schools. Most schools already have teacher collaboration time or a PLC structure. The process of Design Thinking PLCs actually fits into the same expectations as the traditional PLC. PLCs are supposed to focus on the following:

- What do students need to know?
- How will you know if they have learned it?
- What will we do if they have not?

The Design Thinking PLC structure allows teachers to investigate the needs of students and prototype new solutions. Along the way, teachers are constantly investigating what students need to know and what they have learned, and adjusting the prototype to meet the student needs.

In other words, you don't necessarily need to ask permission to adopt Design Thinking PLCs. I have worked with schools that fill out all of the district documentation and adhere to all of the traditional PLC expectations while implementing this new design thinking process.

So you could introduce this as a way to improve your implementation of PLCs, not as a new way to do PLCs. You can do it right now in your current structure and context. Don't rebel against the structure—use it. The Design Thinking PLC process will only make it better.

Administrative Support

Somewhere along the way, some educators started to perceive school administration as having different objectives from teachers. I have even heard teachers refer to administrators as having joined the *dark side* in reference to the evil dark force from the *Star Wars* film series.

And I get it, sort of. I have been a teacher. I have been an administrator. In both roles, I wanted to help students. I still do. But the role of school administrators differs from the role of the teacher. Because of this, it can feel to teachers that some administrators get lost in the numbers and lose focus on the students.

There are good school administrators and bad school administrators, but in my experience, most educators still want to help students. It turns out the Design Thinking PLC was designed for the same purpose.

Having been an administrator, I propose being direct. Tell your administrator that you want to improve your PLC by using design thinking. You can share that the structure supports the work of traditional PLCs. You can share this book and the playbook.

Most administrators support good teaching. They want students to learn. How about a process that focuses on improving learning by meeting student needs? Most administrators will be all in. And if teachers seem on board, excited to adopt the process and try it out, all the better. Bottom-up is always easier to manage than top-down.

The Prototype PLC- A Case Study

You can also live design thinking by being a prototype. You don't have to transform your whole school. If one PLC can start, you can learn what works and what needs to change. You will have evidence of success, what designers call a proof of concept. You can garner buzz and support.

The first time I supported a Design Thinking PLC as a consultant, I shared the idea with the principal. She was excited. She thought that this was just the structure her school needed to move forward. But she was concerned about how to roll it out. She knew this would be a dramatic culture shift for her site, so she wondered how she could start and get teachers onboard.

The next day, a group of eighth-grade teachers came to her office. They were frustrated by what they perceived as a lack of focus and work ethic by the current eighth-grade students. They felt that this year's students weren't working at the same level as previous years. They wanted the administration to do something about it.

The principal saw this as a perfect opportunity to start implementing the design thinking process into the PLCs at the school. She told the teachers if they wanted to support change with these students, she would provide design thinking training for their grade level PLC.

By engaging in the design thinking process, they first interviewed students. Many teachers were not aware that some of their students were experiencing low self-esteem and a lack of connection to their teachers. Instead of fixating on the student behaviors, the teachers started to think about how *they* could change and restructure things to benefit their students. They voluntarily stayed after school for a number of weeks to create three prototypes within three groups.

As they tested these prototypes, they were able to determine what needed to change and what was meeting the students' needs. They designed some great systems to meet the needs statements they had developed. Collaboration increased among the teams outside of structured time as they connected before and after school to check-in on progress and prototype test results. They became a true professional learning community.

Once the eighth-grade team had some data to show from their tests, they shared their results with the rest of the school staff. The administration had set the eighth-grade group up as the prototype for the school in using design thinking as a PLC process. Through this test, the administration had data on how they might reconfigure the school schedule to allow PLCs for this kind of work.

Instead of making structural changes at the beginning and demanding compliance, the administration allowed the prototype group to create data about how those changes would be made. Additionally, the school staff was excited about the prototype, so they wanted more time for this process. It created a bottom-up demand for the structural change.

Even before the eighth-grade team presented their findings to the faculty, there was already a buzz going around the school about the prototypes. Once teachers saw exciting things happening with this prototype PLC, they wanted to be a part of it too.

Be the Prototype

Your PLC can be the prototype. You can start something at your school that will spread like wildfire. You can use design thinking to build something great.

Now you have all of the information you need to revolutionize and transform your PLC into a Design Thinking PLC. You will need to determine your next step. Sure, you will have some speed bumps along the way, but they will not be road blocks.

The opportunity for you to change how you teach using collaborative design thinking awaits. Don't let anything stop you now. You are now part of the Design Thinking PLC movement. Glad to have you onboard. Happy prototyping!

ACKNOWLEDGMENTS

This book is all about collaboration and it wouldn't have been possible without a collaborative effort. Too many people to acknowledge have helped me develop these ideas, but I am grateful for the opportunity to give a few shout outs.

To Kelly, Jack, Cole, Emma, and Dean: You helped me understand the importance of true teamwork. Thanks for always being there for me and keeping me in line.

To Mom and Dad: The ability to innovate is largely dependent on the belief that you can actually create something meaningful. Thank you for instilling that belief in me at an early age and always supporting me.

To Lindsey, Zach, Morgan, and Rachel: My first PLC. Hopefully, I wasn't too bossy. I am thankful for your guidance in my life and incredibly proud to see you building your own teams.

To the teachers and administrators of Hanford Elementary School District: I feel incredibly blessed to have started my educational career in Hanford. So many amazing teachers and administrators showed me what true collaboration was and pushed me to be my best self. Thanks for getting me started!

To the teachers and administrators of the Phillip J. Patiño School of Entrepreneurship: It is difficult to understand the work and effort that goes into creating something completely new. Your tireless commitment and support will never be forgotten. So much of this book is about the work you have started and I hope we can spread it to more schools and teachers around the world.

To the teachers and administrators of Leroy Greene Academy and Entrepreneur High School: Thank you for allowing me to share this framework with you and improve it through your efforts. The prototype has definitely evolved because of your work with students.

ABOUT THE AUTHOR

Supporting innovation in education is what I do. After having opportunities to create unique educational programs at the Phillip J. Patiño
School of Entrepreneurship and the University of the Pacific, I founded
NewSchool Innovation Consulting to share what I have learned with
educators everywhere. This book is the first of a series I hope to write
sharing these frameworks, ideas, tools, and supports.

NewSchool
Innovation Consulting

Whether you are interested in workshops to implement and improve Design Thinking PLCs, or want to create unique educational programs or schools, you can find more about our services at www.newschoolinnovation.com. We offer workshops, webinars, consulting, on-site coaching, and other services to support teacher development and leadership improvement. We are always excited to start conversations about making educational opportunities more engaging and meaningful for students.

Made in the USA
Las Vegas, NV
24 August 2023

76532351R00087